SPECIAL

PRESS COPY

Hello –

I'm sending you this review copy of my new book because you are interested in investment, tax and personal finance topics. For journalists, producers, bloggers and influencers, I hope it is a useful source.

I'm eager to educate investors about taxes, and am available to provide information, quotes, interviews or bylines whenever you need. Contact me at evergreen@hirschleatherwood.com or check out:

evergreenmoney.com/review

I look forward to working with you.

Bill

Bill Harris
Founder, Evergreen Money

PRESS COPY

Investment Tax Guide

How to slash taxes on your investments

By **Bill Harris**

Founder and CEO
of Evergreen Money

Bill is former CEO of PayPal, Intuit and Personal Capital, an investment firm he founded and grew to $25 billion in assets. For ten years, he ran TurboTax, the leading tax software. He has started nine financial technology and cybersecurity companies. Bill believes the digital transformation of financial advice has only just begun.

Investment Tax Guide

How to slash taxes on your investments

The Forgotten Factor

Tax Strategy

Federal Income Tax

Investment Assets

Tax Deductions

Tax Advantaged Accounts

Tax Advantaged Credit

State Income Tax

Afterword

HOW TO USE THIS BOOK. Read the Top Ten Tax Strategies and skim the other sections for topics you are interested in.

EVERGREEN

*I am building a new company called Evergreen Money –
the eighth financial technology company I've founded.
Previous startups include PayPal, One and Personal
Capital.*

*Evergreen is a banking and investment platform that
focuses on maximizing after-tax return and implements
many of the tax strategies described in this book.*

*For book updates and additional articles on investment
taxes, please visit evergreenmoney.com/book.*

Bill Harris
March 2024

It's not what you earn, it's what you **keep**

Tax is the single most important driver of investment performance. By using the right tax strategies, you can slash the taxes on your investments from as high as 50% to as low as zero.

This may surprise you, because no one in the investment industry ever tells you about taxes. Not brokers, not financial advisors, not firms selling mutual funds and ETFs. Everyone talks about *pre-tax* returns – the money you make before you pay taxes. No one talks about *after-tax* returns – the money you actually keep.

> *"Tax is the single most important driver of investment performance."*

Most advisors lack the understanding, products and technology to implement a comprehensive tax strategy. Only the ultra-rich, with armies of tax attorneys, typically benefit from all of the powerful tax strategies I describe in this book.

Taxes can make a profound difference in the true return on your investments. Here is a quick illustration. If you're a single taxpayer at the highest marginal tax rates in a high-tax area like New York City, depending on the type of securities you invest in, you could pay as much as 54.33% in taxes, or as little as 0%.

Top Tax Rates	Ordinary Income				Capital Gains	
	Taxable Interest *	Treasury Bond	Municipal Bond	Triple Tax Free	Qualified Dividends	Capital Gains
Federal	37.00%	37.00%	0.00%	0.00%	20.00%	0.00%
NIIT	3.80%	3.80%	0.00%	0.00%	3.80%	0.00%
NY state	9.65%	0.00%	9.65%	0.00%	9.65%	0.00%
NY city	3.88%	0.00%	3.88%	0.00%	3.88%	0.00%
Total	**54.33%**	**40.80%**	**13.53%**	**0.00%**	**37.33%**	**0.00%**

* Interest from CDs, bank accounts and corporate bonds, *plus* short-term capital gains

"Triple tax free" municipal bonds are exempt from federal, state and local taxes, if purchased by a resident of the state in which the bonds were issued.

Without disciplined tax strategy, capital gains is taxed at 37.3%, the same as dividends. But with tax loss harvesting, gain deferral, margin loans, charitable giving and family gifting, capital gains taxes can be deferred, transferred or eliminated.

There is no better way to improve the performance of your investments than with a disciplined tax strategy. You owe it to yourself to seek out investments and advisors that will minimize the amount that goes to the government and maximize the amount that is available to you and your family.

Money is not a scorecard. It is a precious resource to be used with intention. It is the fuel that gives you the freedom to decide how you want to live, now and for decades to come. Money is a potent tool, but just a tool. It is up to you how to use it.

Are Tax Strategies Legitimate?

Yes. Legislatures write the tax rules to incentivize certain behaviors for reasons of public policy. When you take advantage of a tax strategy – such as using a 529 plan to fund college education – you are acting as they intend you to act.

Judge Learned Hand (yes, that's his real name) famously said "Anyone may so arrange his affairs that his taxes shall be as low as possible ... there is not even a patriotic duty to increase one's taxes."

This book is designed to explain the concepts behind the most valuable tax strategies. In addition, there are chapters covering the basics of taxation of your investments. If you are familiar with the way taxes work, start with the chapter on the Top Ten Tax Strategies. Otherwise, skim through the Federal Income Tax chapter first. You don't need to remember all the rules and rates – just the critical concepts.

"This book explains the concepts."

A quick primer: Our tax system is progressive, meaning that tax rates on the next dollar of income (the "marginal" tax rate) go up as you earn more income. The top marginal federal tax rate (not including state and local taxes) for high-income taxpayers depends on the source of the income.

37% on **ordinary income**, which includes earned income like salary and business income, interest income from bank accounts, CDs, corporate and Treasury bonds (municipal bonds are exempt from federal tax) and short-term capital gains and non-qualified dividends (most dividends are qualified).

– or –

20% on **long-term capital gains** income (you must hold the security for at least one year). Despite the name, this rate also applies to qualified dividends.

– plus –

3.8% for the **Net Investment Income Tax** (NIIT), a federal tax which applies to all investment income for investors with taxable income of more than $200,000 for single filers or more than $250,000 for married filing jointly.

– plus –

13.3% for **state and local** taxes which can run from as low as 0% in states like Texas and up to 13.3% in high-tax states like California.

Putting these parts together, a taxpayer in the top tax bracket in California would pay a total of 54.1% tax on interest income. The top tax rates for residents of New

54.1%

top marginal federal and California tax rate

York City and Portland are a few decimals higher than that.

The starting point to slash your taxes is to take control. Be intentional about the type of assets, vehicles, trades, accounts, and provisions you use. Even if you deploy only a few of the Top Ten Tax Strategies, you'll have more to keep.

Professional Advice

This book does not contain personal tax advice because each individual's tax position is unique. For specific advice related to your own personal financial and tax situation, please work with a tax professional or use tax preparation software.

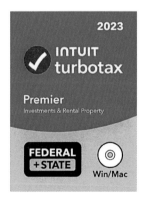

For tax software, I recommend TurboTax, which is used by millions of people each year. It automates the 2,652 pages of regulations in the federal tax code. For the better part of ten years, I used to run the company that makes TurboTax and I can vouch for it as the best consumer tax software available.

The Power of Tax Strategy

In many cases, tax strategy is more important than investment strategy. Yet few investors consider taxes in any depth or detail. Multiple strategies can be used in combination to magnify the tax benefits.

To start with, the type of investment income makes a huge difference in your federal, state and local income taxes (many people forget about the latter two). At the top tax rate in a high-tax area like New York City, you can pay over half of what you earn – up to 54.3% – in total income taxes.

54.3%	40.8%	37.3%	13.5%	0%	0%
Taxable Interest	Treasury Bond	Qualified Dividend	Municipal Bond	Triple Tax Free	Capital Gain*

* As low as 0% if you implement the right tax strategies.

Triple tax free municipal bonds are straightforward – if purchased by a resident of the jurisdiction issuing the bonds, they are exempt from federal, state and local taxes. The disadvantage is that their yields are lower than

Treasuries and corporate bonds, so they only make sense for investors with high tax rates.

Capital gains are the most interesting type of income because, if invested in low or no-dividend stocks, the expected market appreciation is higher than for bonds or dividend-paying stocks. Along with the opportunity for strong growth, there are numerous tax strategies to defer, transfer or eliminate all taxes on capital gains.

An important enabler of these strategies is to hold a large number of individual securities rather than a small number of funds. This provides flexibility to arrange your investments for maximum tax savings. Owning many different stocks and bonds is the foundation for effective tax loss harvesting, gain deferral, charitable giving, annual gifting and asset location.

> *"Move out of old-style investment vehicles like mutual funds."*

This means moving out of old-style investment vehicles like mutual funds, which are high-fee, undiversified and tax inefficient. Even exchange traded funds (ETFs), which are a much better choice than mutual funds because they have low fees and high diversification, do not support the complete tax flexibility that will save you a lot of money.

The obstacle is that designing a well-diversified portfolio of one or two hundred individual assets, then managing all the tax actions throughout the year, is a difficult challenge. So you should look for a financial advisor who offers a fully tax-aware managed account. They are few, but worth finding.

With a team of tech veterans and financial professionals, I am building technology to do this on an automated basis, and so are one or two others. You could think of this as an ultra-personalized tax-minimized version of index investing. I believe this is the future of investing.

But even with today's simpler implementations of disciplined tax optimization, there is much to be gained.

> *"It's the difference between paying over 50% and paying 0% in tax on your investments."*

Is this worth the effort? Yes. Comparing the worst case against the best case, it's the difference between paying over 50% and paying 0% in tax on your investments.

Here are the ten best opportunities to save substantial taxes on your investments. If you are a high-income taxpayer, particularly in a high-tax state, many if not most of these techniques will apply to you.

Top Ten Tax Strategies

1 Tax Loss Harvesting

Harvest tax losses frequently throughout the year using up to hundreds of individual stocks.

2 Tax Gain Deferral

Reduce taxes on appreciated securities using deferrals, offsets and carryforwards.

3 Tax Exempt Securities

Treasury bonds are exempt from state tax. Municipal bonds are exempt from federal and often state tax.

4 Tax Advantaged Accounts

Defer current taxes and compound tax-free with an IRA or 401k. With a Roth, income is tax-free forever.

5 Asset Location

Put the right assets – capital gains vs dividends vs interest-generating securities – in the right accounts.

6 Avoid Short-Term Gains

Eliminate higher taxes on short-term capital gains by managing the holding periods of your investments.

7 Avoid Mutual Funds

Mutual funds are tax inefficient with high fees, low diversification and suboptimal risk/return profiles.

8 Tax-Efficient Credit

Student debt, mortgages, home equity loans and some margin loans are low-cost and tax deductible.

9 Education, Gifts and Estate

Use the annual tax-free transfers to family members and make a plan for inheritances and estate.

10 Donor Advised Funds

Receive charitable deductions and eliminate capital gains tax while controlling the timing of donations.

1 Tax Loss Harvesting

A potent source of tax elimination is to manage your winners and your losers – selling or not selling them at the right time in the right way. Organizing your investments to take full advantage of tax loss harvesting is complicated, but understanding the method is straightforward.

The key concept is that, unlike other types of investments, you have the power to decide if and when to recognize the tax impact. To save taxes, don't sell your winners so you don't pay tax on them, and sell your losers to generate tax losses to offset tax gains when you do sell your winners.

> *"To save taxes, sell your losers but don't sell your winners."*

Here are the basics.

The price of every security – stocks, bonds and funds – fluctuates with the market. When the market price is above the cost basis (the price you paid for it), you have an unrealized *capital gain*. When it is lower, you have an unrealized *capital loss*.

"Unrealized" means that you have not sold the security, so the potential tax gain or loss is not yet recognized for tax purposes. You don't pay tax on unrealized capital gain or loss. When you sell, the gain or loss becomes "realized" and you pay tax on it then.

There are many reasons to sell or not sell a security, but if the only consideration is taxes, it is clear: sell your losers and don't sell your winners. However, once you have sold some losers, you can then sell some winners without paying tax because capital gains and capital losses offset each other.

> *"You can buy back the stock after 31 days without triggering a wash sale."*

If you still want to hold the stock that you sold at a loss, you can buy it back 31 days later and still recognize the original tax loss. If you buy that stock within 30 days, it is considered a "wash sale" and the tax loss is deferred. This is an issue for active or day traders who buy and sell frequently. In addition, frequent trading generates a lot of short-term gain, so don't be a day trader. Particularly after tax, you're more likely to underperform the market than strike it rich.

During most market cycles, you will have more winners than losers, so you will be able to sell only a portion of your winners without paying tax. In this example, if you sold two losers you would have enough loss to offset selling two of the winners, but not the third winner, without paying any tax.

	Cost Basis	Sale Price	Gain/Loss on Sale	Cumulative Gain/Loss
Sell Walmart	$10,000	$8,000	($2,000)	($2,000)
Sell Ford	$10,000	$7,000	($3,000)	($5,000)
Sell Apple	$10,000	$14,000	$4,000	($1,000)
Sell Microsoft	$10,000	$11,000	$1,000	$0
Sell AT&T	$10,000	$12,000	$2,000	**$2,000***

* No tax on the first four sales, but you pay tax on the fifth.

If properly managed, capital gains offer a *triple* tax benefit over interest income. First, the top federal income tax rate on interest (ordinary income) is 37%, while the top tax rate on capital gains is 20%. Second, by deferring or offsetting gains you can reduce the 20% tax to 0%. Third, you simultaneously eliminate all the other related taxes as well – 3.8% for the Net Investment Income Tax and up to 13% in state and local income taxes.

> *"Short-term capital gains are taxed at ordinary income rates."*

There is a wrinkle. Net short-term capital gains – from securities sold less than 12 months after purchase – are taxed at ordinary income rates, which means a total tax on the gain that can run as high as 50%. If possible, *never* sell short-term winners unless you have or can generate enough realized losses to offset the short-term gains.

When to Sell Winners and Losers

Here are typically the best actions for short- and long-term, realized and unrealized, capital gains and losses.

	Unrealized (not sold yet)	**Realized** (already sold)
Short-Term Capital Gain	**Do not sell** until it turns long-term	**Offset** by selling short-term losses
Short-Term Capital Loss	**Sell** to offset short-term gains *	**Use to offset** short-term gains

	Unrealized (not sold yet)	**Realized** (already sold)
Long-Term Capital Gain	**Defer selling** unless offset by losses	**Offset** by selling long-term losses
Long-Term Capital Loss	**Sell** to offset net capital gains *	**Use** to offset net capital gains

* Each year, $3,000 of net capital loss can be used to offset ordinary income like salary

The tax code is a bit more forgiving than outlined above, because you can also offset short-term gains with long-term losses. When filing your taxes, the sequence is (1) offset short-term gains with short-term losses, (2) offset long-term gains with long-term losses and (3) then offset net gains of either type with net losses of the other type.

Each year, you can also deduct up to $3,000 of net capital losses against your other ordinary income, such as salary and business income. This can save up to $1,500 in taxes.

There is one more thing of vital importance – tax lots (different than tax losses). Every time you buy a stock, you create a tax lot. If you buy 10 shares of Apple today and buy another 10 shares tomorrow, you have two different tax lots. Because the market price changes from minute to minute, each lot will have a different cost basis. When you sell, you can sell a whole lot of 10 shares, or a partial lot. The amount of your tax gain or loss depends on which lot you sell.

There are four ways to choose which lot to sell – three of them handled automatically by your broker and a fourth where you have to specify the lot.

- **LIFO.** "Last In First Out" means that the most recently purchased lot is always selected. This is usually the most favorable if you are selling winners, because the older lots have had the most time to appreciate.

- **FIFO.** "First In First Out" means that the oldest lot is always selected. This is sometimes the best automated method if you are selling losers.

- **Average Cost.** This means that the cost basis is always the weighted average cost basis of all the lots you hold of that particular stock. This is usually not the most favorable method.

- **Specific Lot.** This is *always* the best way to sell. It means that for each sale, you choose the specific lot to sell – the lot with the highest loss when selling losers and the lot with the lowest gain when selling winners. That way you can free up the most cash while paying the least tax.

However, the specific lot method requires a lot of attention from you or your financial advisor.

Harvest your losers
Defer your winners

The Best Way to Harvest

Harvesting specific lots is often promised but rarely delivered at its full potential. Here are four approaches to harvesting.

Do-It-Yourself. If you have a self-directed brokerage account, you can review your own holdings – many brokers have a report of realized and unrealized gains and losses available somewhere on their site.

Once a year, typically in December, you can search for losers to sell and winners to sell if you have enough tax loss to offset your tax gains. You can also do this throughout the year, but most people don't have time.

Ironically, robo-advisors **don't** have any advisors

Robo-advisor. A robo-advisor is a digital service that asks six or eight questions to determine your risk profile and then uses simple formulas to invest your money in about ten ETFs. Most robo-advisors promise to harvest losses for you.

However, those ETFs are highly diversified and so their prices are much less volatile than the prices of individual stocks. Because of this, you end up with fewer securities with smaller gains and losses. This sharply limits the value of tax loss harvesting.

Managed account. The very best investment advisors will manually execute tax-lot-specific loss harvesting for you.

Most advisors do not, and those who do tend to serve ultra-rich clients.

A further limitation is that managed accounts often hold mutual funds and ETFs, and that any harvesting is done only once a year in December.

Deconstructed ETF. By far the best approach is to use an ETF-like "indexing" approach, but hold 100 or more individual securities rather than a single ETF. You are certain to have many big winners and many big losers. That's alright because, on average, your return will be the same as if you owned the ETF.

> *"Selling a short-term winner costs up to 50% in taxes. Bring that down to 0% by offsetting with the sale of a loser."*

Over time, you may have multiple lots for each stock. This provides a wide array of tax lots with large percentage gains and losses available for harvesting. To maximize the tax benefits, perform a full harvesting every 31 days, after the wash sale period has expired.

Sometimes called "direct indexing," this is a complicated and time-consuming process, so it is rarely done. As an aside, I am working on a service that will do this automatically.

Regardless of how you harvest tax losses, even if you do it yourself once a year, the tax savings can be significant. Remember, selling a short-term winner can cost up to 50% in taxes, while offsetting the sale of a winner with tax loss from a loser results in *zero* tax.

This first tax strategy is very powerful but complex – that's one of the reasons that most advisors don't do it. The next nine are easier to implement and quicker to describe.

2 Tax Gain Deferral

Harvesting losers is one half of the equation, deferring the gain on winners is the other half. Of course, you don't need to defer the sale of winners you can offset with losses in this taxable year. But for capital gains you can't offset, there are other strategies to defer or eliminate tax on these gains.

The first is easy – just don't sell this year unless you need the money or are convinced the stock will collapse. Remember, the tax hit of selling a *short-term* gain without an offsetting capital loss is so high that, for high-income taxpayers, it will almost always be costlier than bearing a potential decline in price.

Another bonus is that you can carry forward net tax losses from a prior year to the following year and for however long it takes to use them. This is one of the reasons I generally advocate taking losses whenever you can, regardless if you can use them currently or not. You can build a bank of tax losses for the future.

Sometimes, there are opportunities to time your selling. For instance, if you expect your tax rates to be lower next year, hold off recognizing gains until then, or vice versa. And tax rates often go down after you retire, so if you are close to that date, don't sell un-offset winners until then.

If you need the money now, you can also borrow to delay selling a winner until January of the following tax year. More consequential, you can borrow to delay selling a short-term capital gain until 12 months after the purchase.

One of the best ways to borrow for a short period of time is a margin loan. You can borrow up to 50% of the value of your portfolio, and the rates are significantly lower than most other sources of funds. Margin interest is tax deductible against investment income, if the proceeds are used to purchase securities. (See the Tax-Efficient Credit chapter.)

"Tax gain deferral strategies are more effective the more securities you own."

As with tax loss harvesting, tax gain deferral strategies are more effective the more securities you own. You have many more opportunities when you hold 100 individual securities than when you hold the same market value in a single mutual fund or ETF.

The opportunities are further enhanced if you have a "passive" investment philosophy and prefer high diversification versus stock picking. Then you have more freedom to buy and sell any security for tax purposes, rather than worrying about whether you have too much or too little of any particular stock.

My own philosophy is primarily passive, because (1) the tax savings are greater, (2) high diversification reduces risk for the same expected return, (3) unbiased studies have repeatedly shown that active managers, such as stock pickers and market timers, do not outperform the market and (4) active managers charge high fees.

3 Tax Exempt Securities

Most interest, whether from a CD, bank account or corporate bond, is fully taxable when received at high *ordinary income* tax rates. Four types of bonds are exempt from some or all taxes: municipal bonds, "triple tax free" municipal bonds, Treasury bonds and Treasury bills. Each type has tax-saving potential, depending on where you reside.

> **Municipal bonds** (referred to as "munis") are issued by state, county and local governments and are exempt from *federal* tax.
>
> > For mid-term and long-term fixed income in *low-tax* states and in states where triple tax free bond funds and ETFs are not available
>
> **Triple tax free municipal bonds** are issued by state, county and local governments. They are exempt from federal tax and – for residents of the issuing municipality – exempt from *state and local* tax as well.
>
> > For mid-term and long-term fixed income in *high-tax* states

Treasury bonds are issued by the federal government and are exempt from *state and local* tax.

>For mid-term and long-term fixed income in *high-tax* states when municipal yields are relatively low

Treasury bills are *short-term* (typically four-week to 26-week) obligations issued by the federal government and are exempt from state and local tax.

>For short-term cash in *high-tax* states

For high-income taxpayers, tax-exempt bonds are better than corporate bonds with similarly high credit ratings.

>*"To compare bonds, use the tax-equivalent yield."*

To compare bonds, use the tax-equivalent yield, which means the pre-tax yield a taxable bond would have to pay to produce the same after-tax yield as a tax-exempt bond. The formula is:

>*tax-exempt yield / (1 – tax rate) = tax-equivalent yield*

Here is a simple example. For someone with a 50% total tax rate on ordinary income, a triple tax free muni with a 3% yield would have a 6% tax-equivalent yield.

>3% / (1-50%) = 6%

Here is the comparison:

> $100,000 in a triple tax free muni with a **3%** pre-tax yield and a 0% tax rate earns $3,000 after tax.

> $100,000 in a taxable corporate bond with a **6%** pre-tax yield and a 50% tax rate earns $3,000 after tax.

The biggest disadvantage of municipal bonds is that their pre-tax yields are low, so they don't make sense for people with low to moderate marginal tax rates. But for people with high incomes – particularly in high-tax states like California and even in no-tax states like Texas – municipal bonds are typically the best choice for longer-term high-quality fixed income exposure. (These pre-tax yields are illustrative.)

	Pre-Tax Yield	Tax-Equivalent Yield California	Texas
Corporate Bonds	4.6%	4.6%	4.6%
Treasury Bonds	4.4%	5.1%	4.4%
Municipal Bonds	2.9%	4.9%	4.9%
Triple Tax Free Munis	2.9%	6.3%	4.9%

Four caveats. First, this comparison is only valid for corporate bonds with the highest credit ratings – AAA and AA. Lower quality bonds, and particularly high-yield or "junk" bonds, have higher "default risk" and therefore higher pre-tax yields. Despite the added risk, they should be a part of your portfolio, and there are no tax-exempt alternatives – no low-quality Treasuries and few low-quality munis.

Second, it usually does not make sense to buy individual bonds or build a "bond ladder" – it's cumbersome, time consuming and insufficiently diversified. When choosing between bond funds and bond ETFs, pick a low-cost well-diversified, highly liquid ETF.

Third, bonds and bond funds carry significant risk even if they are government backed. The longer the duration (how long until the bond matures) the greater the "interest rate risk." When interest rates go up the price goes down. When interest rates go down, the price goes up.

> *"For short-term cash, use United States Treasury bills."*

Finally, for short-term cash, use United States Treasury bills (there are no short-term munis or corporate bonds). T-bills are high-yield and exempt from state taxes. They provide higher tax equivalent yield than CDs or online high-yield savings accounts, and massively higher yields than savings and checking accounts at major banks.

	Pre-Tax Yield	Tax-Equivalent Yield California	Texas
US Treasury bills	5.4%	6.2%	5.4%
High Yield Savings	5.0%	5.0%	5.0%
High Yield Savings	4.5%	4.5%	4.5%
Regular Bank Savings	0.2%	0.2%	0.2%
Regular Bank Checking	0.1%	0.1%	0.1%

"US Treasury bills are guaranteed by the full faith and credit of the United States."

For a California resident in the top marginal bracket, money put in Treasury bills will double in value in a bit over 20 years. Putting money into a regular bank savings account will yield almost nothing.

As of this writing, the Treasury bond yield curve is inverted, meaning that the 5.5% shorter-term rates are higher than the 4.4% longer-term rates. Shorter-term T-bill rates are often compared to the "Fed Funds" rate, currently 5.5%, which is the rate banks can borrow from the Federal Reserve.

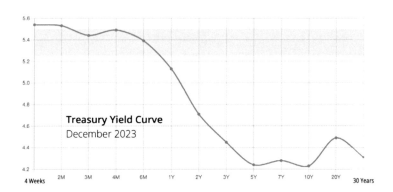

Treasury Yield Curve
December 2023

Treasury bills are generally considered one of the safest investments available. T-bills have no interest rate risk because they are ultra short term. T-bills have no default risk, because they are guaranteed by the full faith and credit of the United States.

The challenge is how to own them. Buying small amounts of Treasury bills on the secondary market and then rolling them over every four to eight weeks is difficult. For now, the best option is a short-term Treasuries ETF.

The drawbacks are (1) you'll pay an expense ratio of 10 to 40 basis points (0.1% to 0.4%), (2) most short-term Treasury ETFs maintain average maturities of one to three years, which exposes you to interest rate risk and (3) it's up to you to claim the tax exemption, a problem that few people are aware of.

Some people don't get the tax benefit they expect from a Treasury mutual fund or ETF. That's because of the way they are reported on the IRS Form 1099-INT – the year-end tax statement you receive from your broker.

Brokers report the interest from individual Treasury bonds on Box 3 of the tax statement, and tax software automatically handles the exemption. However, Treasury bond funds and ETFs do not typically invest 100% in Treasuries, so all of the interest is reported on Box 1, along with the non-tax-exempt interest.

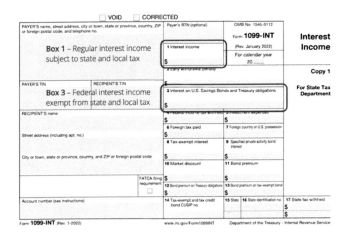

You, your financial advisor or your tax preparer need to go to the website of the fund provider, look up the percentage invested in Treasuries for that specific fund, and manually input that information into the tax software. Even if you remember this manual step, you still only get an exemption on that percentage of the interest, which can range from 99% down to 50% depending on the fund or ETF.

> *"T-bills are the holy grail of high-yield, tax-exempt, risk-free, instantly-available money."*

The good news is that some financial firms are building solutions to make investing variable amounts of money directly in T-bills quick and painless. In the future, you will be able to keep your short-term cash directly in Treasury bills, providing the holy grail of high-yield, tax-exempt, risk-free, instantly-available money.

4 Tax Advantaged Accounts

Tax deferred and tax exempt accounts have multiple tax benefits and, if you are not yet retired, should usually be a key part of your long-term investment plan.

Tax deferred accounts are tax-deductible on the way in and taxable on the way out.

- 401k (403b, 457b and TSP in the public sector)
- Individual Retirement Account (IRA)
- Simplified Employee Pension (SEP)

Tax exempt accounts are not tax-deductible on the way in but are tax-free on the way out.

- Roth 401k
- Roth IRA and "backdoor" Roth IRA

With tax deferred accounts, your contributions are locked up until age 59½. Early withdrawals incur a penalty of 10% of the withdrawn amount (exceptions include withdrawals for certain medical and educational expenses). Tax exempt Roth accounts are less restrictive because you can withdraw amounts you contributed (but not earnings on those amounts) before 59½ without penalty.

If you are satisfied you will not need the money before age 59½ or you like the notion of enforced savings (which you should), then make full use of tax advantaged retirement accounts. To start with, if your employer offers a 401k plan, take advantage of the "employer match."

Free Money

 Most employers who sponsor a 401k plan also offer an employer match, meaning they will match your contribution with an additional contribution of their own. A strong 401k program will match as much as 50 cents on the dollar, on up to 6% of your salary.

This is free money. Take it. It's like an instant 50% return on your investment. Always contribute to your 401k up to the match, but not necessarily more than that.

> *"It's like an instant 50% return on your investment."*

If your employer offers a 401k plan, the best strategy is generally to contribute in the following sequence:

1. Contribute to your 401k **only up to the employer match** – after that, an IRA offers more flexible and lower-cost investment options.

2. Contribute to a traditional or Roth IRA up to the annual contribution limit of $7,000 if under 50 and $8,000 if over 50 (unless you are further limited by income phase-outs).

3. Then, if you still want to contribute more, you can max out your 401k up to the annual contribution limit of $23,000 if under 50 and $30,500 if over 50.

Except to get the employer match, it is better to hold your assets in an IRA than in a 401k. IRA's generally have lower costs, better investment options, and are more flexible for implementing tax strategies such as asset location. You can't move funds out of the 401k of your current employer, but once you are no longer working there, you should roll over your "orphaned" 401k balance into your IRA. (Some people lose track of old 401k accounts and never recover their money.)

Unfortunately, it is tricky for higher-income taxpayers to contribute to an IRA or Roth IRA.

- The tax deductibility of contributions to a traditional IRA is phased out if your taxable income (AGI) is greater than $87,000 if single or $143,000 if married filing jointly.

- Your ability to contribute directly to a Roth IRA is phased out if your taxable income (AGI) is greater than $161,000 if single or $240,000 if married filing jointly.

- However, there is no income restriction when doing a "backdoor Roth IRA." Step one is to make a *nondeductible* contribution to a traditional IRA (up to the $7,000/$8,000 annual limit). Step two is to make a tax-free conversion into a Roth IRA. This is the primary method by which high-income taxpayers can contribute to an IRA

If you are self-employed and don't have access to a 401k, you should generally contribute to a traditional or Roth IRA first, then contribute to a SEP. The tax advantages of SEP plans are similar to 401k plans, but the rules are different. You must be self-employed or own a small business, and all contributions must be made by the business rather than by the employee. The annual contribution limits of a SEP are the lesser of 25% of your compensation from the business or $69,000.

To Contribute or Not to Contribute?

Always contribute up to the full employer match in a 401k to get your free money. What are the benefits of contributing beyond that amount?

In all scenarios except early withdrawal, a tax advantaged account significantly outperforms a taxable account. When the tax rate is held constant at 40% over a 20-year period, both tax deferred and tax exempt accounts outperform a taxable account by 70%. This is due to the tax-free compounding.

	Taxable Account	Tax Deferred 401k, IRA, SEP	Tax Exempt Roth IRA	
		Constant 40% Tax Rate		
Current Income	10,000	10,000	10,000	
Current Tax Rate	40%	0%	40%	← Roth IRA
Amount Invested	6,000	10,000	6,000	taxed at start
Pre-Tax Return	7.0%	7.0%	7.0%	
Compounding Tax Rate	40%	0%	0%	← Tax-free
After-Tax Return	4.2%	7.0%	7.0%	compounding
20-Year Growth	7,662	28,697	17,218	
Pre-Tax Withdrawal	13,662	38,697	23,218	
Withdrawal Tax Rate	0%	40%	0%	← 401k, IRA, SEP
After-Tax Withdrawal	13,662	23,218	23,218	taxed at end
Benefit vs Taxable Account		**70%**	**70%**	

The percentage benefit increases as the marginal tax rate increases above 40% and as the time period lengthens beyond 20 years.

Tax exempt accounts pay tax at the start of the period and tax deferred accounts pay tax at the end of the period. As long as the tax rate remains constant throughout the period, both tax deferred accounts (401k or IRA) and tax exempt accounts (Roth 401k or IRA) deliver the same end result.

To Roth or Not to Roth?

The tax advantages of a Roth IRA or Roth 401k are different from those of a traditional 401k and IRA account.

	Tax Deferred 401k, IRA or SEP	**Tax Exempt** Roth 401k or Roth IRA
Employee Contributions	Contribution is tax deductible	Contribution is **not** tax deductible
Investment Returns	Returns compound tax free	Returns compound tax free
Distributions in Retirement	Withdrawals taxed as ordinary income	Withdrawals after 59½ are **tax free**
Required Minimum Distributions	RMDs starting at age 73	No RMDs - compound indefinitely
Treatment for Inheritance	Pay full tax at death of last spouse	Inherit tax free if Roth opened >5 years ago

Although they both have the same end result if the tax rate is constant, most taxpayers can expect their tax rate to be lower in retirement. In this case, a tax deferred account will significantly outperform a tax exempt account.

If the tax rate is 40% at the start and throughout the compounding period but decreases to 25% at the time of withdrawal, the tax benefit of a tax deferred account increases to 112%.

	Constant 40% Tax Rate			25% at End
	Taxable Account	Tax Deferred 401k, IRA, SEP	Tax Exempt Roth IRA	Tax Deferred 401k or IRA
Current Income	10,000	10,000	10,000	10,000
Current Tax Rate	40%	0%	40%	0%
Amount Invested	6,000	10,000	6,000	10,000
Pre-Tax Return	7.0%	7.0%	7.0%	7.0%
Compounding Tax Rate	40%	0%	0%	0%
After-Tax Return	4.2%	7.0%	7.0%	7.0%
20-Year Growth	7,662	28,697	17,218	28,697
Pre-Tax Withdrawal	13,662	38,697	23,218	38,697
Withdrawal Tax Rate	0%	40%	0%	25%
After-Tax Withdrawal	13,662	23,218	23,218	29,023
Benefit vs Taxable Account		**70%**	**70%**	**112%**

Benefit of tax *deferred* account increases
if the tax rate is lower at time of withdrawal

A Roth account does not benefit from a lower tax rate at withdrawal, because the tax was already paid at the start. Nevertheless, there are six reasons you might want to use a Roth.

- If your income precludes a *deductible* contribution to a traditional IRA, contributing directly to a Roth IRA or indirectly through a backdoor Roth IRA is your only option.
- If you are not in your peak earning years and/or expect significant investment income in retirement, your tax rate may be lower now than later and a Roth would yield a superior result.
- Unlike a traditional 401k or IRA, you can withdraw an amount equal to your contributions without an early withdrawal penalty.

- There is no maximum age for contributions to a Roth IRA, so you can continue to add to your tax-free assets later in life.
- There are no required minimum distributions (RMDs).
- Upon your death, whomever inherits your Roth 401k can make tax-free withdrawals.

Second, for affluent families, the best thing about a Roth is its flexibility, particularly if you do not anticipate needing distributions while you live. There are no required minimum distributions so you can keep compounding tax free indefinitely and you can bequeath a Roth account to your children without losing its tax-free status.

The direct benefits of tax advantaged accounts are potent. But there is a second layer of tax benefit when you use them as part of an asset location tax strategy. For more on that, turn to Tax Strategy #5, Asset Location.

5 Asset Location

At least as important as having the right investments, is putting the right investments in the right place. It can make a large difference in the taxes you pay.

For instance, if you manage it correctly, you can pay zero tax in a taxable account on a stock that does not pay dividends. Paradoxically, that same stock in an IRA will eventually be hit with ordinary income tax at a rate that can exceed 50%.

Your entire portfolio has investments generating *interest* income, *dividend* income and *capital gain* income. Be careful which you put where. There are three categories of investment accounts:

- **Taxable.** Regular individual and joint accounts
- **Tax Deferred.** 401k, IRA, and some other accounts
- **Tax Exempt.** Roth IRA, 529 plans and some other accounts

For long-term investments of a decade or more, deferred and exempt accounts are a tremendous opportunity. But only if you use them wisely. Here are the basic principles.

> First, fill up your tax deferred and tax exempt accounts with *interest*-generating assets like bonds.

Second, if you still have capacity in the tax advantaged accounts, fill them further with *dividend-generating* assets like high-dividend stocks.

Finally, keep your *capital gain-generating* assets in your taxable accounts.

Why? Interest income is taxed at higher ordinary income rates, which can be 50% or more including state and local taxes. So this is the most valuable income to defer or exempt.

Dividends are taxed at lower capital gains rates – still up to 30% or more including state and local taxes – but you don't have the opportunity to harvest, defer or transfer dividends. You always pay tax on dividends when they are received. Stocks that pay dividends can also generate capital gains, so they are in the middle. If you have additional room in your tax advantage accounts, add your highest-dividend stocks.

> *"Capital gain assets should not be held in tax deferred accounts."*

Securities that generate only capital gains should not be held in tax deferred accounts for three reasons. First, you don't benefit from harvesting and deferral techniques inside a 401k or IRA.

Second, when these stocks are eventually distributed, they are taxed at ordinary income rates and you've just converted a low-tax asset into a high-tax asset.

Third, if the capital gain-generating asset is in a tax advantaged account, you can't eliminate tax on the appreciation with charitable giving, family gifting, or stepped-up basis.

Many people do this exactly wrong. They think of tax advantaged accounts as long-term vehicles (which they are) so they put their long-term assets (stocks) in those accounts. Instead, you should manage your investment portfolio as an integrated whole, and use tax structures to maximize your overall after-tax result.

If you have the wrong mix of assets in your accounts, you can often fix it without incurring much tax liability. You can sell capital gain-generating assets in your tax deferred account and buy capital gain-generating assets in your taxable account with no tax consequence. And you can sell interest-generating assets that do not have much unrealized gain in your taxable account and buy interest-generating assets in your tax deferred account without incurring much taxable gain.

Again, why put the right assets in the right accounts? Putting an interest asset in a taxable account could change it from a 0% tax rate to a 50% tax rate. And putting a capital gain asset in a tax-deferred account could change it from a 0% tax rate to a 50% tax rate. You lose in both directions.

6 Avoid Short-Term Gains

Never sell a winner with a short-term capital gain unless you can offset it with capital losses.

A gain on any security or other property you sell within 12 months of the purchase date is a short-term capital gain. Short-term capital gains are taxed at higher rates than long-term capital gains. The federal tax rate on short-term versus long-term capital gains is 10% versus 0% at lower incomes and 37% versus 20% at higher incomes.

Here are the total marginal tax rates on short-term capital gains for various incomes in various states.

Single Filer	Federal	NIIT	State	Total
$200k Income Taxpayer in a High-Tax State (CA)	32.0%	3.8%	9.3%	45.1%
$200k Income Taxpayer in a No-Tax State (FL)	32.0%	3.8%	0.0%	35.8%
$1 Million Income Taxpayer in a High-Tax State (CA)	37.0%	3.8%	13.3%	54.1%
$1 Million Income Taxpayer in a No-Tax State (FL)	37.0%	3.8%	0.0%	40.8%

In almost all circumstances, the tax penalty for selling a winner in less than a year substantially outweighs the risk of a potential decline in price during whatever remains of that period. (If you believe that no one can reliably out-think the market on highly researched, publicly traded securities, as I do, then the only risk is market risk, not stock-specific risk.)

The exception is when you can offset your short-term capital gains with capital losses, but even then you are using tax losses that might be better utilized in the future.

The exception to the exception is that if you have a *net* capital loss (your total capital losses exceed your total capital gains across both short- and long-term), you can deduct up to $3,000 of these losses against other ordinary income, such as salaries, bonuses and business income. This saves taxes at the higher ordinary income rates and is more valuable than using the short-term losses to offset long-term gains or to offset against short-term capital gains that you could convert to long-term capital gains by delaying their sale.

The management of net short-term capital losses can become complicated. To simplify, *never* sell short-term winners unless you have a compelling reason to do so.

7 Avoid Mutual Funds

The first mutual funds were started in the 1920's, but they did not take off until the mainframe computer revolution in the early 1970's. This is when IBM computers made it possible to compute the daily NAV (the end-of-day price at which mutual funds are bought and sold) before the next sunrise.

Computers ushered in the era of *mass production* of investment funds, which allowed ordinary citizens to participate in the stock market. This, in turn, unleashed a torrent of equity financing for companies which has supercharged the American economy to this day. This is the single biggest innovation in capital markets since the introduction of brokerage accounts themselves.

However, after a 50-year run, mutual funds are now obsolete. The problems are threefold.

High fees. Despite significant reductions in fees over the decades, the cost of mutual funds remains stubbornly high. The expense ratio (the fees) of most mutual funds is a half percent to a full percent or even more.

Poor risk/return. Because most mutual funds are actively managed, they typically hold about 50 stocks as opposed to 500 stocks held in an S&P 500 ETF. If those stocks have a similar "beta" (a measure of the risk in a specific stock compared to the market as a whole), then the expected return on 50 stocks will be the same as on 500 stocks.

However, because there are fewer stocks to average out the swings in price, 50 stocks will be more volatile than 500 stocks. Because risk is measured by volatility, mutual funds carry higher risk for the same expected return. This is called "uncompensated risk."

> *"The worst problem with mutual funds is tax inefficiency."*

Tax inefficiency. The worst problem is tax inefficiency – you'll pay more taxes on the same securities. This is due to high turnover and the obstacles to utilizing tax strategies.

The average turnover ratio of actively managed mutual funds is about 0.75. This means that about 75% of their holdings are sold and replaced every year. This is because (1) mutual fund managers are making bets on individual stocks rather than holding stocks for the long-term and (2) some managers engage in "window dressing," the practice of selling unloved stocks and buying hot stocks before the end of each quarterly reporting period.

With a mutual fund, not only do you recognize gains and losses when you sell the fund yourself, you also get the gains and losses of stocks sold by the managers *within* the fund. High turnover ratios mean that most of these distributed gains are short-term gains – the worst kind.

Most consequential is the inability to use many tax strategies with mutual funds. Because you own one big fund rather than many individual stocks, you don't have many big winners and big losers so there are much fewer harvesting and deferral opportunities. Asset location and gifting or charitable giving of highly appreciated securities is also hamstrung.

Exchange Traded Funds are Better

Exchange traded funds (ETFs) are superior to mutual funds in all three ways.

ETFs have low fees which range from about 0.1% to about 0.4% depending on the fund provider and the size and liquidity of the index being tracked. Because of high diversification, ETFs do not generate uncompensated risk. And, although they are not ideal from a tax perspective, at least they do not suffer from the high turnover and distribution of *within-fund* capital gains like mutual funds.

Personally, I love ETFs for their low fees and high diversification. My industry hero is Jack Bogle, who founded Vanguard and single-handedly dragged a recalcitrant investment community towards index investing. As a result of decades of steadfast advocacy of his heretical ideas, Vanguard is now one of the two largest asset managers in the world. (I was lucky to work with Jack before he passed.)

"But there is something even better than an ETF, and that is a managed account"

Managed Accounts are Best

But there is something even better than an ETF, and that is a managed account. If well executed with advanced technology – which, unfortunately, they rarely are – managed accounts offer the low fees and high diversification of index funds and add unlimited personalization and powerful tax opportunities. Older technology enabled *mass production* through mutual funds, and the latest technology is enabling *mass customization* through managed accounts.

There are two types of managed accounts. Traditionally, a broker or portfolio manager creates a "model" of 50 stocks they think will beat the market, puts all their clients in the same model, and manages for pre-tax performance ignoring the specific tax issues of each client.

The modern way is to start with an index-like portfolio of individual securities and then personalize and optimize from that highly diversified foundation.

Many of the tax strategies in this book cannot be fully implemented if you hold mostly mutual funds and ETFs. The key to unlocking potent tax opportunities is building a balanced portfolio of a large number of individual stocks.

Individualized portfolios have more flexibility to pursue tax opportunities because they are free from a list of specific stocks and can manage the portfolio at a higher level, ensuring high diversification and overall conformance with the factor targets. They can also be highly personalized for each individual investor.

I believe that factor-based managed accounts, utilizing specialized software to deliver low cost, high diversification, customized construction and full tax benefits, are the way all high-income investors should invest.

8 Tax-Efficient Credit

Most households have outstanding credit of some type, whether it's a credit card or a mortgage. But many people don't manage their credit to optimize the impact on their finances. Managing your credit has two components: how much and what type, which is where taxes come in.

How Much Credit?

Most people think of saving and investing as two separate things, but they are intimately connected. The most effective way to increase your investment assets over the long term is to save more now.

The foundation of a successful financial life is simple: ***spend less than you make.*** Unless you are in retirement and excluding emergencies and special purchases, you must maintain a positive cash flow from regular recurring income and expenditures. Without this, you will fail.

Positive cash flow is the only way to reduce debt and fund retirement. Set a target to save 20% of your income each year, with a *minimum* of 10%. A popular rule of thumb is "50/30/20" – 50% for housing and basic necessities, 30% for discretionary spending, and 20% for savings. If you can't sustain regular savings of at least 10%, adjust your lifestyle.

Exceptions include emergencies and special purchases. The most common and devastating emergency is an unexpected medical crisis, which can quickly run into tens of thousands of dollars, or even  more if it becomes a chronic issue. If you are not prepared, this can turn into a financial crisis as well. So be prepared:

- Always maintain comprehensive medical insurance with full coverage for extraordinary high-cost issues, even at the expense of accepting a high deductible for less extreme problems. A tax-deductible Health Savings Account (HSA) is a good idea as well.

- Have an emergency fund of liquid assets sufficient to cover six months of living expenses.

- Exercise, eat well and don't smoke. This lessens the risk of diabetes, cancer, strokes and heart disease. Poor health is also a *financial* issue.

The other common emergency is the loss of a job. If this happens, give yourself one month to decompress, then get back to work. Take freelance or even gig work if you can't find a new job right away – it is important to maintain the habit of working five days a week. Have a six-month emergency fund, but try not to use it.

Special purchases include cars, homes and education.

Automobile. Don't buy a new car until you are saving 20% of your income. Simply don't.

Home. Don't buy a new home until you can put at least 20% down. Don't buy a home as an investment – it's not. For many people, particularly young mobile individuals and families, it is better financially to rent. Partly due to increased interest rates, in some cities, the average cost of buying is now as much as 50% higher than the cost of renting.

Don't buy a *second* home until you can (1) pay the interest and often-underestimated maintenance costs and still save 20% of your income and (2) put at least 50% down. That's much higher than most financial advisors will tell you, but financial leverage is a recipe for trouble.

Having said that, if you have a family and are settling down in one area for at least five years, a long-term home is one of the best life decisions – and financial decisions – you can make. Unlike a new car for which studies show increased overall happiness for only 30-60 days, a comfortable home in a pleasant neighborhood can provide a lifetime of pleasure and satisfaction.

Education. For yourself or your children, education is the best investment you can make, but only if you or they are serious about it. It is one of the most expensive purchases you will ever make. Figure on

$100,000 per person for a college education, not including the student's loss of income for a good part of four years. For many, financing an education while in school results in ten years of heavy debt. It is wiser to save for the education in advance.

What Type of Credit?

Almost as important as how much credit is what *type* of credit. Most people know what types are better, but many don't act on that knowledge.

Just like investments, tax is an important and often-forgotten piece of the puzzle. The least expensive forms of credit are secured by some form of collateral (government collateral in the case of student loans) and are tax deductible. The most expensive are unsecured and not tax deductible.

You pay taxes on interest you *earn*. If it is tax deductible, you save taxes on interest you *pay*.

Here are some very approximate pre-tax and after-tax costs of different types of debt, in an environment of a 5% "Fed Funds" rate (the rate at which the Federal Reserve lends to banks) such as we are in today.

Type of Debt	Pre-tax Interest Rate	After-tax Interest Rate
Student	5-8%	3-5%
Mortgage	7-9%	4-6%

Home Equity	8-10%	5-6%
Margin	9-12%	7-10%*
Auto	10-15%	10-15%
Personal	15-30%	15-30%
Credit Card	20-30%	20-30%
Overdraft	Infinity?	Infinity?

* Some margin loans are tax deductible in some cases. See the chapter on Tax Advantaged Credit for more details on all types of credit.

The types of credit that are tax-deductible are student loans, mortgages, home equity loans and some margin loans.

Student loan interest is deductible whether you itemize or not – it is an "above-the-line" deduction – but the deductibility is phased out starting at $85,000 of taxable income (actually, modified AGI) for single filers and at $165,000 for taxpayers who are married filing jointly.

The amount of interest you can deduct for student loans is capped at $2,500 per year. If you took out the loan recently, this is about what you would pay on a $50,000 loan. Nevertheless, student loans, particularly those subsidized by the federal government, are often the least expensive loans you can get, even without the tax benefit.

Mortgages are the classic example of tax deductible low-cost credit. But there are some requirements.

- You must itemize your deductions.

- You can only deduct interest on the first $750,000 of mortgage debt on your primary and secondary residence.
- You can deduct the points paid to get the loan, which is similar to prepaid interest.

Mortgages are by far the largest source of consumer debt in America.

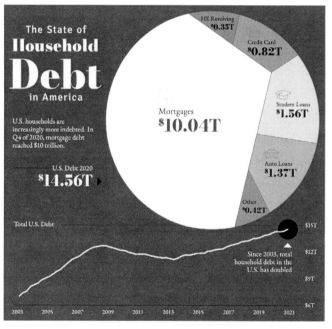

Source: New York Federal Reserve

Home equity debt is tax deductible in the same way as mortgages and is included in the same $750,000 limit, provided the proceeds are used to buy, build or remodel a primary or secondary residence. Interest rates are slightly higher than for a mortgage.

Home equity loans are term loans with fixed amortization schedules and are good for longer term lending. Home equity lines of credit (HELOCs) are better for shorter term or variable needs.

Margin loans are secured by your stocks and bonds and carry reasonable interest rates. You can typically borrow up to 50% of the market value of your marginable assets, and will have to pay down the loan if the balance drops below 50%.

Margin loans are tax deductible against investment income if used to purchase other securities, but generally not if they are used for other purposes. (There is a technique that uses "tracing rules" to get the tax benefit for other uses, but it is beyond the scope of this book.)

Tax-Efficient Credit Strategy

In general, the objective is to minimize (though not always) and prioritize (always) your debt. Here is your optimal credit strategy:

1. Don't pay off student loans early. Always pay what is due but no more. Particularly if the loan was taken a while ago at lower rates, if it was taken directly from the government, if your marginal tax rate is high, and/or if the interest does not exceed the $2,500 annual limit, it is the most favorable credit you will

ever have, with a true after-tax cost as low as 3%. Even if you have no other debt, you can invest the funds in Treasury bills and earn 5%, taking home a net 2% pre-tax spread on the interest.

2. The same is often true for mortgage loans. Particularly if you have an older mortgage with pre-tax rate as low as 3% and an after-tax rate as low as 2%, do not pay it off early. Of course, you must have the discipline to build an offsetting balance in low-risk liquid assets.

3. If you are regularly carrying higher-cost debt like credit card debt, a home equity loan often makes sense as well. HELOCs are particularly well suited for variable or unpredictable needs, and it's not a bad notion to put a HELOC in place, even if you don't need the money now. It's a great source of low-cost tax-deductible credit in an emergency.

4. Refinancing an existing mortgage is an interesting option if you need the money, but less so now that interest rates have risen. By refinancing a partially-paid-down mortgage, you are effectively converting what would have been non-deductible credit card debt into deductible and lower-cost mortgage debt.

5. Even though it is tax deductible, I would rarely suggest using a margin loan to purchase securities –

that's just adding to your financial leverage. However, as a method to raise cash for other short-term or emergency purposes, it is a good source of credit. Not only is it low cost, it is easy to get. It can take months to secure a mortgage and weeks to secure a home equity loan, but it takes only days to secure a margin loan. Margin loans generally do not require a credit check. Your brokerage account probably already allows margin lending and, if not, it's easy to add.

6. Car loans are higher-cost and not deductible but they are better than credit card debt. However, the best solution is not to buy an expensive new car until you can pay cash. And don't be fooled, an auto lease is really just an auto loan with a higher embedded interest rate.

7. Personal unsecured loans are high cost and not tax deductible. The primary reason to use them is if you have no other way to reduce perpetually revolving credit card debt. The better solution is to reduce your expenses.

8. Don't pay interest to your credit card, let your credit card pay interest to you. There are three types of credit card users: transactors, revolvers and those who dip in and out of debt usage. Everyone knows that revolving credit card debt is wildly expensive – typically over 20% and without deductibility. But if

you are a transactor and pay off the full balance before the due date every month, the credit card company is giving you the "float" – effectively a free loan equal to an average of 40 days of your credit card spending. It is important to pay off the balance consistently because, even if you don't pay it off in full for just one month, you will also be charged interest retroactively on the prior month's purchases.

9. Don't use overdraft. It is actually more expensive than a payday loan, and it is a sign you are not paying attention to your money.

"The same simple principle applies: maximize your after-tax yield."

Think of credit as a form of investment – "negative investment." Whether you are going from 3% to 6% after-tax yield on your investments or from –20% to –3% after-tax yield on your negative investments (credit), the same simple principle applies: maximize your *after-tax* yield.

9 Education, Gifts & Estate

There are numerous tax efficient ways to give money to your children, family members and others close to you. You can pay for their education, transfer money on an annual basis, and bequeath cash, securities and property when you pass.

529 Plan

A 529 plan is the tax-efficient way to pay for educational expenses from kindergarten through graduate school, for your children, your friends, or even yourself.

It functions similarly to a Roth IRA, except that the funds are for education rather than retirement: you do *not* get a federal tax deduction for your contribution, but the earning compound tax-free and any withdrawals are tax-free if used for qualified educational expenses. There are no time limits, the beneficiary can be switched to any other family member, and after 15 years any unspent balance up to $35,000 can be rolled over tax free into a Roth IRA.

Disadvantages of a 529 plan are that the investment options are usually limited to mutual funds and ETFs (choose low-cost ETFs), and the fees are higher if you purchase through a broker than if you purchase directly from the 529 plan itself (purchase directly from the plan).

Each state offers its own plan with different features and costs but you can usually purchase a plan from any state. Some state plans offer state tax deductions on the contributions to residents of that state. There are four locations where this is especially valuable.

State or City	Maximum Joint Deduction	Annual Value at Top Tax Rate	15-Year Value at Top Tax Rate
New York City	$10,000	$1,353	$29,188
New York state	$10,000	$965	$20,823
New Jersey	$10,000 *	$1,075	$23,197
Washington DC	$8,000	$860	$18,558

* per taxpayer who earns less than $200,000

Notably, other high-tax states like California, Oregon and Hawaii do not offer meaningful state tax deductions.

However, except in cases such as the death or disability of the current recipient, if you withdraw the funds for any other purpose, you must pay tax on the compounded earnings *plus* a 10% penalty. 529 plans are a great deal if there is a high likelihood that your child or another family member can use the money for education. If not, and if you don't live in one of the high-tax states listed above, the 10% early withdrawal penalty and lack of flexibility make it an unattractive option.

Gifts

There are numerous ways to give money to your children, family members or friends without incurring a gift tax.

First, gifts to pay for tuition or medical expenses, gifts to political organizations, and gifts to your spouse are exempt.

Second, gifts between spouses are exempt.

Third, you can give up to $18,000 to any other person each year without incurring a gift tax. You and your spouse can each give that amount to each child, so for a family with three children, you and your spouse can give up to $108,000 per year.

Fourth, any gifts above those amounts will not incur gift tax up to the amount of your lifetime gift and estate tax exemption. This is a single amount that combines what you can give away during your lifetime or upon your death without incurring gift and estate tax. If you give more than $18,000 to anyone in one year, your lifetime exemption is reduced by that amount.

> *"Give money to your children ... without incurring a gift tax."*

The federal lifetime exemption is $13.61 million in 2024, reduced by any gifts you have made in excess of the $18,000 annual exclusion. This is the amount you can use to offset taxes on your estate.

Estate

After parents have a new child, they often think about saving for the child's education. But the most important thing you can do is have a well-drafted will and living trust that makes arrangements for your family in your absence.

Estate planning is extremely complex and highly personalized. If you have a high net worth, you need an experienced advisor who specializes in this area. Although no substitute for professional counsel, here are a few high-level observations.

Your estate must pay up to 40% federal estate tax on the amount the taxable estate exceeds the lifetime exemption. For example, let's assume you have a $20 million estate. If you had previously given away $1.0 million in excess of your annual gift exclusions, your remaining lifetime exemption would be $12.61 million ($13.61 million minus $1.0 million). Then your federal estate tax would be about $2.96 million ($20 million minus $12.61 million, times roughly 40%).

For married couples, both spouses receive the $13.61 million exemption, for a total of $27.22 million. An estate planning attorney can set up a living trust (or "revocable" trust) to maximize the value of this spousal benefit. A living trust with a pour-over will can also get your estate out of probate, which makes the execution of your estate faster, less costly and more private.

Twelve states and the District of Columbia have their own estate tax, with tax rates as high as 20% and exemptions as low as $1 million.

2023 State Estate Tax

	Estate Tax Rates	Estate Tax Exemption
Connecticut	12.0%	$12,920,000
DC	11.2 - 16.0%	$4,528,800
Hawaii	10.0 - 20.0%	$5,490,000
Illinois	0.8 - 16.0%	$4,000,000
Maine	8.0 - 12.0%	$6,410,000
Maryland	0.8 - 16.0%	$5,000,000
Massachusetts	0.8 - 16.0%	$2,000,000
Minnesota	13.0 - 16.0%	$3,000,000
New York	3.06 - 16.0%	$6,580,000
Oregon	10.0 - 16.0%	$1,000,000
Rhode Island	0.8 - 16.0%	$1,733,264
Vermont	16.0%	$5,000,000
Washington	10.0 - 20.0%	$2,193,000

Importantly, estates benefit from a type of tax forgiveness called "stepped-up basis" at death. This means that any assets owned by the deceased, including stocks, bonds, real estate and personal property, is revalued to the "fair market value" at the time of death.

For instance, the cost basis of appreciated securities is automatically increased to the current price, erasing any unrealized capital gain and permanently eliminating tax on that gain. Later in life, it makes sense to hold (not sell) stocks that have dramatically increased in value over the years. If sold before death, those capital gains taxes have to be paid.

It works the other way for unrealized losses. At death, stocks that have fallen in price are "stepped-down," or revalued at the current price. This destroys the valuable tax losses that would otherwise have been available. However, if the securities with unrealized loss are sold before death, those losses can be used to offset other taxes due.

While giving appreciated stock to charities has multiple tax benefits, gifting appreciated stock is not always the optimal path for non-charity recipients. The recipient will inherit the low cost basis and the unrealized capital gain, whereas, if that appreciated stock was passed through an estate, the potential tax would disappear.

These revaluations at time of death reinforce the twin strategies of tax loss harvesting and tax gain deferral. From a tax point of view, sell your losers whenever you can and hold your winners as long as you can.

10 Donor Advised Funds

The ultra-rich often create their own foundations for charitable giving now and as a legacy for the future.

Traditional foundations are effective tax vehicles, but they are too costly and complicated for most of us to create and administer. There is now a better solution called a *donor advised fund* or "DAF," which delivers almost all the benefits of a traditional foundation at a fraction of the cost, time and trouble. I call it a "personal foundation."

Here are some of the benefits of a donor advised fund versus a traditional foundation.

- No IRS and state documentation and registration
- No annual federal and state tax filings
- No board of directors and professional staff
- May give anonymously
- Higher annual contribution limits as a percent of your taxable income (AGI)

Here are two reasons why traditional foundations are less attractive from a financial point of view.

- Foundations must distribute at least 5% of their assets each year. DAFs have no minimum distribution requirements.
- Foundations must pay a 1.39% excise tax on net investment income and realized capital gains. DAFs pay no taxes.

Donor advised funds are easy, flexible and low-cost, while traditional foundations have no such virtues. This is the only instance I know where regular investors have an advantage over the ultra-rich (although they are also starting to use DAFs).

Why Donate to Charity?

There are many philanthropic and tax-related reasons to do charitable giving. From a philanthropic point of view, it is an opportunity to support the groups and causes you are committed to, and to build a legacy for yourself and your family.

You can donate your time by volunteering or your financial resources by giving. Studies consistently show that spending on charitable activities has a larger impact on your own satisfaction and happiness than spending on material goods. We are social animals and thrive on helping each other.

> *"We are social animals and thrive on helping each other."*

From purely a *tax* point of view, charitable giving has a double benefit. First, you can deduct donations of cash or the fair market value of marketable securities, like stocks, bonds and funds. This deduction is only available if you itemize your deductions and is generally limited to 60% (but in some cases less) of your table income ("AGI"). In extreme cases, it may trigger the Alternative Minimum Tax, which is too complicated to discuss here but now impacts a very small number of taxpayers – fewer than 200,000 in the US.

Second, if you donate appreciated securities, you never pay capital gains tax on the unrealized gain. This is a great way to eliminate all taxes when you sell your winners.

Assume you hold a stock with a $10,000 market value that has doubled in value and has an unrealized gain of $5,000.

Assume you are a high-income taxpayer in a high-tax state, with a marginal tax rate of 50% in federal, state and local taxes on ordinary income and 35% on long-term capital gains.

If you donate the stock to charity and itemize your deductions, you receive a charitable deduction of $10,000 which, at a 50% rate, is worth **$5,000.**

You also eliminate capital gains tax on the unrealized appreciation of $5,000 which, at a 35% rate, is worth **$1,750.**

You just reduced your tax bill by **$6,750.**

Importantly, you have to transfer the securities into a DAF (or directly to a charity) for them to sell. If you sell the securities and donate the cash proceeds, you have to pay tax on the capital gain.

Why Use a Donor Advised Fund?

If you decide to donate to charities, a donor advised fund is the best way to do it.

> *"If you donate to charities, a donor advised fund is the best way to do it."*

Without a DAF, donating securities is difficult and cumbersome, and some small charities are not able to accept donated securities. Even they prefer to do it only for larger gifts. For donating $100 to your school, cash is the only practical option. With a DAF, you tell the sponsoring institution how much to give to whom and they take care of the rest, including keeping tax records and receipts for you.

Without a DAF, you have to make a charitable contribution and decide where it goes at the same time. With a DAF, you can make a contribution to your DAF at any time, such as the end of the tax year, and get the tax deduction immediately. Then, the money can sit in the DAF earning tax-free returns until you decide how much and to whom to give.

You no longer own the assets in your DAF, but you effectively control them and can allow other family members to help decide where and when to give.

Federal Income Tax

Six income types, three federal tax structures, eleven federal tax rates, four filing statuses – plus state taxes – determine your income taxes

The United States collects more than 40% of its total revenue from income taxes compared to 25% in other developed countries. The tax brackets are progressive, meaning that the marginal tax rate increases as your income increases.

Your marginal tax rate is higher than your effective (average) tax rate. Investment income is taxed *after* earned income, so an additional dollar of investment income is always taxed at your highest tax bracket and can push up both your marginal and effective tax rates.

For tax purposes, all income is not the same. Depending on the type of income, the type of account, what you make and where you live, the combined federal, state and local tax on $1,000 of income could be anywhere from $0 to $541 – a punishing tax rate of 54%.

Most investors (and most financial advisors) focus on pre-tax return. That's a mistake. Interest rates are up, but if taxes take half of what you earn, your assets have to work twice as hard just to catch up. In fact, the higher inflation and interest rates go, the more you fall behind on your investments – a 50% tax doesn't make much difference when rates are 1%, but it does when rates are 5%.

Let's break it down. In order of importance, the major drivers are (1) the type of income, (2) the type of account receiving the income, (3) your taxable income, (4) your filing status and (5) your city and state of residence.

There are two major federal individual income tax rate structures, each with different rates and tiers.

Ordinary income rates range from 10% to **37%**
Long-term capital gains rates range from 0% to **20%**

There are six major types of taxable income. The top rates for long-term capital gains and most dividends are much lower than for other types of income.

Type of Income	Tax Rates
Earned income	Ordinary income (37%)
Interest	Ordinary income (37%)
Qualified dividends	Long-term capital gain (20%)
Non-qualified dividends	Ordinary income (37%)
Long-term capital gain	Long-term capital gain (20%)
Short-term capital gain	Ordinary income (37%)

In addition, high-income taxpayers pay the Net Investment Income Tax (NIIT) – an additional 3.8% on all types of investment income, but excluding earned income like salary, wages and income from active businesses such as proprietorships, partnerships and small business corporations (subchapter S corporations).

The difference between the top ordinary income rates and long-term capital gain rates, as well as the ability to time the sale of capital gain assets like stocks, create powerful opportunities to reduce your taxes.

> *"You could pay up to 54.1% tax on the interest from your bank account."*

How punishing can taxes get? If you are single in California with taxable income of a million dollars or more, you could pay up to 54.1% tax on the interest from your bank account.

Federal top ordinary income tax rate	37.0%
Net Investment Income Tax	3.8%
California top income tax rate	13.3%
Total tax rate	**54.1%**

California has the highest marginal state income tax rate in the country. Another eight are 8-11%, most are 4-8%, and seven have zero income tax, the largest being Florida and Texas.

On the federal side, tax rates are progressive, meaning the tax rate increases on each successive tier of income. Here are the federal tax brackets for the 2024 tax year. Each tier has a tax rate that is applied to the income up to the highest threshold in that tier.

For instance, a single taxpayer with $50,000 of ordinary income would pay 10% on the first $11,600, plus 12% on the next $35,549 ($47,149 minus $11,600), plus 22% on the next $2,851 ($50,000 minus $47,149).

Federal Income Tax Rates
Rates apply to income between that bracket and the next highest bracket

2024 Tax Rates	Single Taxpayer	Married Filing Jointly	Married Filing Separately	Head of Household
Ordinary Income				
Earned income, interest, non-qualified dividends and short-term capital gains				
10.00%	$0	$0	$0	$0
12.00%	$11,600	$23,200	$11,600	$16,550
22.00%	$47,150	$94,300	$47,150	$63,100
24.00%	$100,525	$201,050	$100,525	$100,500
32.00%	$191,950	$383,900	$191,950	$191,950
35.00%	$243,725	$487,450	$243,725	$243,700
37.00%	$609,350	$731,200	$365,600	$609,350
Long-Term Capital Gain				
Long-term capital gains and qualified dividends				
0.00%	$0	$0	$0	$0
15.00%	$47,025	$94,050	$47,025	$63,000
20.00%	$518,900	$583,750	$291,850	$551,350
Net Investment Income Tax (NIIT)				
All sources of investment income except municipal bonds				
0.00%	$0	$0	$0	$0
3.80%	$200,000	$250,000	$125,000	$200,000

Filing Status

Your filing status does not change the tax rates, but it does change the income brackets at which you pay those rates. There are four major filing statuses, plus a fifth for qualifying widows or widowers.

> **Single.** If you are unmarried or legally separated on the last day of the year
>
> **Married Filing Jointly.** If you are married and both you and your spouse agree to file a joint return.
>
> **Married Filing Separately.** If you are married and one or both spouses want to be responsible for only your own taxes.
>
> **Head of Household.** If all these are true:
> 1. You are unmarried or legally separated on the last day of the year.
> 2. You paid more than half the cost of keeping up a home for the year.
> 3. A qualifying person lived with you in the home for more than half the year.

Most people file as single or married filing jointly. Some married couples elect to file separately if (1) they are managing their money independently (2) they don't have confidence in their partner's financial discipline, or (3) they both have substantial incomes, in which case filing separately can result in a lower tax bill. To compare your taxes under these two filing statuses, you can use tax software such as TurboTax.

Earned Income

All forms of cash compensation for work you perform personally is subject to federal income tax at *ordinary income* tax rates. This includes salary, wages, bonuses, commissions, tips, gig work, freelance income and self-employment income.

Up to 85% of your Social Security retirement benefits are included in earned income if your taxable income exceeds these thresholds.

Single taxpayers

0% if your income is less than $25,000
50% if your income is $25,000 to $34,000
85% if your income is over $34,000

Joint taxpayers

0% if your income is less than $32,000
50% if your income is $32,000 to $44,000
85% if your income is over $44,000

If you have gig work payments, freelance income and self-employment income, you can deduct or make tax adjustments for business-related expenses. These include expenses for:

- Home office
- Education related to your business
- Health care premiums
- Retirement plan contributions
- Rent, insurance and other business expenses
- Travel and entertainment
- Automotive expenses

If you are self-employed and work from home, you can deduct home office expenses – this is *not* available for people who work remotely and are on an employer's payroll. If you use part of your home *exclusively* as your principal place of business, you can use the simplified method of $5 per square foot up to 300 square feet – or $1,500.

Or, the more complex method is to calculate the square footage of the office area as a percentage of the area of the house. Then take that percentage of the costs of maintaining your home, including real estate taxes, mortgage interest, rent, repairs, utilities, insurance and depreciation.

> *"Many gig workers and freelancers fail to deduct legitimate business expenses."*

Automotive deductions are especially important for Uber and Lyft drivers (or anyone who uses their car in their line of business), who can deduct gasoline, insurance, repairs, lease payments and depreciation. Or, instead, they can simply claim the standard IRS mileage deduction of 65.5 cents per mile.

Many gig workers and freelancers fail to deduct legitimate business expenses from their taxable income, which can cost them thousands of dollars.

To claim any of these deductions, you must keep records and receipts and file a Schedule D and other forms with your tax return. Tax software will automatically fill out these forms.

Payroll Tax

Compensation as an employee of a business, often referred to as "W-2 income," is subject to payroll tax to support Social Security and Medicare, plus additional state tax in some states. Calculating payroll tax is complicated, but your employer does the calculation for you on your W-2.

The federal payroll tax is up to 15.3% of individual compensation, half paid by the employer and half paid by the employee. Your portion is up to 7.65% and consists of:

> **Social Security**
> 6.2% on compensation up to $160,200

> **Medicare**
> 1.45% on all compensation
> (plus *additional* 0.9% on compensation over $200,000)

If you are self-employed, you must pay the entire 15.3% by yourself because you are looked at as both the employee and the employer.

It is an unusual feature of the US tax system that earned income is taxed at higher rates than investment income.

> *"The total tax on earned income can*
> *be staggering – up to 67.1%."*

Let's take the most extreme example – a single filer in the highest tax bracket in Portland, Oregon. Including employer and employee payroll taxes and federal, state and local income taxes, the total tax on earned income can be staggering – up to 67.1% on your last dollar of income.

Federal income tax	37.00%
Oregon state income tax	9.90%
Portland income tax	4.00%
Employer payroll tax	7.65%
Employee payroll tax	7.65%
Medicare surcharge	0.90%
Total tax	67.10%

For every dollar a high-income Portland taxpayer earns, he or she will keep 32.9 cents.

Interest

Interest income is taxed at ordinary income rates. This includes bank accounts, certificates of deposit, money market funds, bond funds, corporate bonds, high-yield bonds (also known as junk bonds), foreign bonds, business and personal loans, and other interest-paying instruments.

Interest is taxable on the date it is received (in certain instances such as short-term Treasury bills and zero-coupon bonds, if the interest payment is not received until the following year, it is taxable when it is accrued).

> *"US Treasuries are exempt from state and local income taxes."*

However, US Treasuries are exempt from state and local income taxes. In no-tax states like Texas and Florida, this doesn't make a difference. But in high-tax states like California and New York, this can save you up to 13.3% in state taxes.

Due to changing market conditions and company expectations, bonds can produce capital gains or losses in addition to interest income. For instance, the market value of a bond goes up when interest rates go up, and down when rates go down. If you sell a bond for a gain, that portion of the income is capital gains.

Treasury bills have maturities from four weeks to one-year, Treasury notes from two to 20 years, and Treasury bonds from 20 to 30 years. Both notes and bonds pay interest every six months, while T-bills are "zero-coupon" bonds that accrue interest based on the difference between the price when you purchase and the price when you sell.

Because Treasuries are guaranteed by the full faith and credit of the United States, they are generally considered the safest place for your money. Due to their relative safety, high interest rates versus bank accounts, and state tax exemption, these are excellent vehicles for storing available cash.

> *"Treasuries are guaranteed by the full faith and credit of the United States."*

Unlike bank deposits for which FDIC protection is limited to $250,000 per depositor, the government guarantees Treasuries to an unlimited amount. Treasuries also have massive liquidity – more so than any other asset in the world.

Municipal bonds issued by towns, cities, counties and states are exempt from federal income taxes. However, because of this tax benefit, municipals pay lower interest rates than corporate bonds and only make sense for high-income taxpayers. They also have very low liquidity, so they are best suited for long-term buy-and-hold investments.

If your tax residence is within the issuing municipality, the interest may be exempt from state and local taxes as well. For instance, there are triple-tax-free bonds available in California and New York City – areas with some of the highest tax rates in the country.

Dividends

Qualified dividends are taxed at beneficial long-term capital gains rates which range from 0% to 20%. *Non-qualified* dividends are taxed at higher ordinary income rates, which range from 10% to 37%.

Qualified dividends are from domestic corporations and foreign corporations traded on a US exchange.

> *"Qualified dividends are taxed at the beneficial long-term capital gains rates."*

Dividends from a corporation are taxed at much lower rates than interest on bonds from the same corporation. Of course, stocks carry higher risk and greater volatility than bonds.

Dividends enjoy the same low tax rate as capital gains from holding the stock for one year or more. However, the tax is due when the dividends are paid, as opposed to capital gains which are not taxed until the asset is sold.

Because you can usually control the timing of selling assets with unrealized capital gain or loss, this unlocks substantial tax benefits from strategies like tax loss harvesting, tax gain deferral, charitable giving and estate planning.

Capital Gains

When you sell a stock, mutual fund, ETF, investment real estate or other investment asset, you realize capital gains on the difference between the sales price and the original purchase price, or the cost basis.

Long-term capital gains are the most advantageous type of income from a tax point of view because (1) long-term capital gains tax rates are much lower than ordinary income rates, (2) you can choose when to sell and recognize the gain or loss, (3) capital gains can be offset by capital losses to eliminate taxes on the sales and (4) there are permanent deferral methods, such as charitable contributions and stepped-up basis in an estate.

> *"Holding a stock for 12 months results in a 10% to 17% higher after-tax return."*

Long-term capital gain rates are capped at 20%. However, assets sold within one year or less generate *short-term* capital gains or losses, which are subject to much higher ordinary income tax rates. It is particularly important not to sell as you approach the end of the 12-month holding period. Holding a stock for at least 12 months results in a 10% to 17% higher after-tax return from the same pre-tax gain.

Federal Tax Only	Lower Income	Higher Income
Short-term capital gain	$1,000	$1,000
Ordinary income rate	10%	37%
Net Investment Income Tax	0%	3.8%
After-tax return	$900	$592
Long-term capital gain	$1,000	$1,000
LT capital gains rate	0%	20%
Net Investment Income Tax	0%	3.8%
After-tax return	$1,000	$762
Long-term vs short-term	+ $100	+ $170
Percentage increase	+ 10%	+ 17%

Because you can choose when to sell, you can convert short-term into long-term capital gain, but you can deploy other tax strategies as well.

 Your winners and losers are a Rubik's cube of gains and losses. Securities you've already sold during the tax year have generated *realized* gains and losses, while those you haven't sold have *unrealized* gains and losses. Realized and unrealized gains and losses can be short-term or long-term.

Capital gains and losses create a blizzard of tax reduction opportunities. Let's assume you don't feel committed to any individual security – that you are willing to buy, sell or hold any stock or fund. If so, here are some tax tactics:

- Hold securities with unrealized short-term gains for at least a year to convert them to long-term gains
- Sell unrealized short-term losses to cover any realized short-term gains
- Sell unrealized long-term losses to cover the sale of assets with unrealized long-term gains
- Defer selling selling assets with unrealized capital gain to postpone taxes due

At the end of the tax year, IRS rules require you to (1) offset realized short-term losses against short-term gains, (2) offset realized long-term losses against long-term gains and (3) offset the resulting net realized short-term and long-term gains against each other.

While realizing short-term capital gains is costly, realizing short-term capital losses can be beneficial, because you can deduct the first $3,000 of short-term capital losses against other ordinary income each year.

Most people do not manage the timing of their capital gains. Those who do, typically do so in an imprecise manner at the end of the year. But the best method is to actively harvest tax losses every month.

If you do sell a security at a loss, do not buy that same security for 30 days. Otherwise, it is considered a wash sale, and the tax loss resulting from that sale will be deferred.

Any excess of losses over gains in one year can be carried forward to offset gains in future years, so the tax reducing value of capital losses never expires.

Net Investment Income Tax

The Net Investment Income Tax (NIIT), also known as the "Obamacare Tax", applies to all investment income (but not earned income like salary and wages), including interest, dividends, capital gains, royalties and passive net rental income (after subtracting operating expenses but not financing costs).

However, the NIIT only applies to taxpayers with taxable incomes over these amounts.

- $200,000 – single

- $250,000 – married filing jointly
- $125,000 – married filing separately
- $200,000 – head of household

The NIIT is a flat 3.8% tax that is added on your federal income tax rate on the lesser of (1) your net investment income or (2) the amount by which your modified adjusted gross income (MAGI) surpasses the thresholds above.

The **greatest** financial and tax vehicle ever devised for employees

Stock Options

The best companies want to share their success with their employees and the best employees want to work where that success is shared. There are multiple ways to participate in the growth of the equity of the company you work for:

- Incentive stock options (ISOs)
- Non-qualified stock options (NSOs or non-quals)
- Restricted stock units (RSUs)
- Employee stock purchase plan (ESPP).

Incentive stock options, the type most employees receive from early-stage companies, are the greatest financial and tax vehicle ever devised for employees. You receive 100% of the gains if the stock price increases, bear none of the losses if the stock price falls, and put up no money to participate.

ISO's are a form of compensation, but there is no tax upon grant, vesting or exercise (in limited circumstances, you might be subject to the Alternative Minimum Tax upon exercise on the "spread" between your original strike-price and the FMV of the stock). Only if the stock goes up and you sell your shares do you pay tax, only on the gain, and only at capital gain rates if you have held the shares at least one year from exercise and two years from grant (otherwise, ordinary income rates apply).

Non-qualified stock options, the only type available to non-employees and to highly-compensated employees for a portion of their options, are similar except the gain is taxed upon exercise at the higher ordinary income rates. Here is how stock options work.

> **Stock options** are your right to purchase common shares of a company, typically valid for ten years or three months if you leave the company.

> **Grant date** is the date you are awarded the stock options, although they cannot be exercised and sold until they vest.

> **Vesting schedule** is the period of time you must work at the company to own your options, typically 1/48th vesting every month for 48 months (four years).

Exercise price is the price per share you must pay to exercise your options and purchase the shares.

Current price is the market price for a public company or the fair market value per share as determined by the board for a private company.

After they vest, options become valuable when the current price is higher than the exercise price, or when there is a realistic possibility that it will be in the future. In a public company, you can exercise and sell your shares at any time. In a private company, there are limited occasions to sell your shares so optionholders typically wait to exercise. With an ISO, it is advantageous to exercise well before you want to sell, to start the one-year holding period necessary to get capital gains tax treatment when you sell.

Larger companies with lower growth potential often offer restricted stock units instead. With an RSU, you are granted shares that vest over multiple years and you earn the entire value of the shares – not just the gain – as they vest. However, you also pay tax on the entire value as they vest at ordinary income rates, plus Social Security, Medicare and state income tax. RSUs are more similar to deferred cash compensation than to stock options.

With an employee stock purchase plan, a company lets its employees purchase company stock at a discount. Politely decline. These plans are complicated and carry risk of loss. You already have enough eggs in your company's basket – like your job and your salary – so diversify your portfolio and invest elsewhere. Options and RSUs are free; purchasing company stock is not.

Two great tax benefits: the mortgage interest deduction and the gain exclusion upon a sale

Residences

Owning a home is like owning any other asset, but with two great tax benefits: the mortgage interest deduction and the gain exclusion on the sale of your primary residence.

Homeowners can deduct the interest on up to $750,000 of mortgage loans on their first or second homes and, in many instances, the points on the mortgages as well. This deduction has greatly increased in value since mortgage rates spiked – an older mortgage at 3% on $750,000 is a $22,500 deduction while a recent mortgage at 7% on $750,000 is a $52,500 deduction.

Because a mortgage is secured by the house, it is a low-risk, low-interest source of long-term borrowing. The tax deductibility makes it the second-most favorable type of loan. (See the Tax-Efficient Credit chapter.)

The interest on a home equity loan may also be deductible if you use the proceeds to buy, build or substantially improve your home, if the loan amount plus your mortgage are no more then $750,000. However, you must itemize deductions to qualify to deduct the interest from a mortgage or a home equity loan.

If you sell your primary residence, you can exclude from taxable income the first $250,000 of gain if you are single or the first $500,000 of gain if you are married and filing jointly. This exclusion is not available for second homes and may only be used once every two years. Remember to track the money you spend on substantial improvements because that will increase your tax basis and lower the capital gains tax on the sale.

Alternative Minimum Tax

Prior to the Tax Cuts and Jobs Act in 2018, many taxpayers were caught up in the alternative minimum tax. Now, only about 200,000 taxpayers are subject to the AMT. The major items likely to trigger the AMT are (1) high household income, (2) large capital gains that are not offset by capital losses and (3) large incentive stock option exercises. Luckily, you often control the timing of the second and third factor.

Proprietorship, Partnership & Corporation

Small businesses can be corporations, partnerships, or sole proprietorships. Income from corporations is taxed at business tax rates within the corporation, and then taxed again when cash is distributed to the shareholders.

Partnerships and LLCs provide liability protection but pass through all revenues and expenses directly to the tax returns of the partners *without* a double layer of taxation. Most freelancers, gig workers and self-employed business owners operate as a "sole proprietorship," meaning all their business revenues and expenses are part of their personal tax return on Schedule C.

Many consultants, freelancers and independent contractors forget to deduct work-related expenses from their personal tax return. Overlooked expenses can include travel, meals, phone, internet, supplies and home office expenses. For instance, Uber drivers can deduct the cost of operating their vehicle.

Estate Tax

For most people, the lifetime gift and estate tax exemption will eliminate any federal tax on your estate. The lifetime exemption allows you to make aggregate gifts and bequests of up to $13.61 million for a single taxpayer and $27.22 million for married taxpayers filing jointly without paying any federal estate tax. (Note that the lifetime exclusion is scheduled to decrease to $5,000,000 on January 1, 2026 unless the higher allowance is extended by Congress.)

However, twelve states and the District of Columbia have their own estate taxes with tax rates as high at 20% and exemption amounts much lower than the federal lifetime exemption. See the State Income Tax chapter.

Separately, the annual gift exclusion allows any individual to give up to $18,000 per year to any other individual tax free. Each parent can give $18,000 to each child (or anyone else), so a family with three children can give six times $18,000, or $108,000 without taxes to the parents or the children.

Estate planning is one of the most complex areas of personal finance and generally outside the scope of this book. If you have a multi-million dollar net worth, you need professional estate planning advice.

Investment **Assets**

*Your risk profile and asset allocation are the
starting points for designing an optimal portfolio*

The foundational portfolio
decision is asset allocation –
the percentage allocated to
stocks, bonds and cash
equivalents.

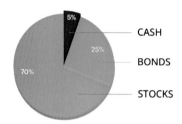

- **Stock** subclasses include domestic and international,
  growth and value, higher dividend and no dividend,
  large cap and small cap, and industry sectors.

- **Bond** subclasses include corporate, high-yield,
  foreign, Treasury, and municipal.

- **Cash** equivalent subclasses include bank accounts,
  CDs and money market funds (corporate, Treasury
  and municipal).

Most funds and advisors build portfolios around risk profiles
alone. **Most forget about the other driving factor – tax.**

Traditionally, your risk profile is set based on your age, income, wealth and "time horizon" – how long will it be until you need the money. The primary factor is age, because the conventional wisdom is the older you are the more "conservative" your portfolio should be, meaning more bonds and less stocks.

Old-fashioned brokers use the "Rule of 100" under which the percentage stock should equal 100 minus your age. If you are 40 you should have 60% stocks and if you are 70 you should have 30% stocks.

This age-based approach is inadequate. It ignores everything else that makes each investor unique. Not only is it overly simplistic investment theory, it also ignores behavioral finance research. Not all 45-year-olds want the same thing, nor should they have the same thing.

"Tax is the single most important driver of true investment performance."

Even so, the bigger missed opportunity is tax. Most funds and advisors trumpet pre-tax returns and ignore taxes. For most affluent investors, tax is the single most important driver of true investment performance. Because asset allocation determines the tax characteristics of the securities in your portfolio, it has an outsized influence on tax efficiency.

As an extreme example, $10,000 interest from a corporate bond generates as much as $5,000 in tax, while a $10,000 unrealized gain on a stock generates none.

UP TO 50%
federal, state and local tax rate

If you are in the top tax bracket in California, New York, New Jersey, Oregon, Hawaii, Minnesota, Massachusetts or the District of Columbia – states representing a quarter of the US population – you will pay more than 50% tax on any interest you receive from corporate bonds, money market funds, bank accounts and CDs.

ZERO
federal, state and local tax rate

If, on the other hand, you hold appreciated stocks that pay no dividends, you will pay no tax on the unrealized gain until you decide to sell them. You can delay selling until the next tax year, or use various tax strategies to defer the tax indefinitely or even eliminate the tax liability.

In order of the most tax-efficient asset classes to the least, here are the major investment types.

1. Municipal bonds, bond funds and bond ETFs
2. Individual stocks – no dividend
3. Individual stocks – higher dividend
4. Treasury bonds and bills
5. Exchange traded funds
6. Mutual funds
7. Corporate bonds, bond funds and bond ETFs

8. Individual stocks – short-term, if sold in 12 months
9. CDs and bank savings accounts
10. Cryptocurrency

The income tax on individual stocks which pay no dividends can be deferred, transferred or eliminated. The tax on your CD is up to 50% or more.

The Bulls and Bears of Wall Street

You will always have winners and losers. Take advantage of the volatility with tax loss harvesting and gain deferral.

Individual Stocks

Stocks generate four types of income. From best to worst, they are (1) long-term capital gains, (2) qualified dividends, (3) short-term capital gains and (4) non-qualified dividends.

The maximum federal income tax rate on long-term capital gains is only 20% (but up to 37% after adding NIIT, state and local taxes in locations like California and New York City). However, you can decide how and when to sell or dispose of the stock, providing numerous opportunities to defer, transfer or eliminate tax on the gain. From a tax point of view, this is the very best type of income.

Qualified dividends are taxed at the same federal long-term capital gains rate. However, you cannot control the timing of receipt of dividend income. Therefore there is no escaping taxation in the tax year which they are paid.

Short-term capital gains on stocks sold within 12 months of purchase are subject to ordinary income tax rate, the same as salary and bonuses. For a high-income taxpayer at the top tax bracket in California or New York City, the total tax burden is over 54%. Do whatever you can to avoid recognizing short-term capital gains unless they can be offset with capital losses.

Non-qualified dividends are taxed when paid at ordinary income rates rather than at lower long-term capital gain rates. The good news is that most dividends from public stocks (but not money market funds and ETFs) are qualified, as long as:

- You have held the shares for more than 60 days during the 121-day period that begins 60 days before the dividend is paid
- You have not hedged the shares with puts, calls, or short sales

Primarily because of the opportunities to manage capital gains, individual stocks create a playground for powerful tax strategies. They play a central role in eight of the Top Ten Tax Strategies.

✓   Tax Loss Harvesting
✓   Tax Gain Deferral

Tax Exempt Securities
- ✓ Tax Advantaged Accounts
- ✓ Asset Location
- ✓ Avoid Short-Term Gains
- ✓ Avoid Mutual Funds
 Tax-Efficient Credit
- ✓ Education, Gifts and Estate
- ✓ Donor Advised Funds

Exchange Traded Funds

ETFs upended the market for pooled investment vehicles like mutual funds.

Exchange Traded Funds

Exchange traded funds (ETFs) are the third most consequential innovation in consumer investing, behind the brokerage account and the mutual fund. ETFs use an "index" investment policy in which the portfolio follows a broad market index such as the S&P 500; as opposed to mutual funds which follow an "active" investment policy which invests according to the decisions of the fund manager.

ETFs have caused a revolution in the investment world and it is due to one man – Jack Bogle of Vanguard. Unbiased academic studies have long shown that active management does not produce statistically significant risk-adjusted long-term performance. Jack pounded this simple realization into the heads of investors.

ETFs have grown rapidly to 30% market share versus mutual funds, and last year $900 million was withdrawn from mutual funds and $600 billion was invested in ETFs. Vanguard became the largest manager of consumer investments in the world – larger than Fidelity, Schwab or Merrill Lynch. This demonstrates the public's growing understanding that index or passive investing is generally superior to active investing, at least in highly liquid public markets.

There are numerous non-tax factors that make ETFs attractive.

- **Lower Fee.** Because ETFs don't incur the personnel and research costs of active management, the fees charged by ETFs (also known as the "expense ratio") are much lower – 5-50 basis points* per year for an ETF versus 50-100 basis points for a mutual fund.

- **Lower Risk.** ETFs hold a highly diversified portfolio of all the stocks in its index – for example, a S&P 500 ETF holds 500 stocks. An active mutual fund typically holds 50-100 stocks, delivering lower diversification and higher volatility for the same type of assets.

- **Lower Complexity.** Buying and holding ETFs is easy. You don't have to listen to sales pitches by fund companies or advisors touting one manager over another, make or accept decisions without meaningful information, or track the performance of each mutual fund against the market – an ETF tracks the market all by itself.

* A basis point equals one one-hundredth of a percent, so 1.0% equals 100 basis points.

There are also tax benefits of an ETF versus a mutual fund.

- Capital gains *within* an ETF are not taxed (though capital gains when your sell the ETF there are)
- Because the underlying index rarely changes, ETFs have low turnover which reduces trading and administrative costs.

However, there are important tax *limitations* of an ETF versus individual stocks, based on the fact that you own only one large security with relatively small price movement rather than many small securities with many large upward and downward swings in value.

> *"There are important limitations of an ETF versus individual stocks."*

This makes tax optimization more challenging and less effective because you don't have many ingredients to work with. Without big winners and (hopefully fewer) big losers, the tax value of loss harvesting, gain deferral, asset location and many asset disposal strategies is severely limited.

Use of ETFs rather than individual stocks significantly diminishes the power of seven Top Ten Tax Strategies.

     ✗   Tax Loss Harvesting
     ✗   Tax Gain Deferral
         Tax Exempt Securities
     ✗   Tax Advantaged Accounts
     ✗   Asset Location
     ✗   Avoid Short-Term Gains
         Avoid Mutual Funds
         Tax-Efficient Credit
     ✗   Education, Gifts and Estate
     ✗   Donor Advised Funds

ETFs follow a public or proprietary index, of which there are many. There are many ETFs that track the same sector or the same index, such as the S&P 500 or the NASDAQ. A common question is whether there are too many ETFs.

Too many ETFs?

There are 8,754 ETFs – three times the number of stocks listed on the New York Stock Exchange.

ETFs have been a tremendous step forward for individual investors. But you can significantly improve your true after-tax investment performance with individual stocks. The current obstacle is that rigorous execution of some of the tax strategies using individual stocks is still a manual process, but automated solutions are on the way.

Mutual Funds are Less Tax-Efficient than ETFs

They have high turnover, which generates short-term gains at ordinary income rates.

Mutual Funds

Mutual funds are one of the worst structures in which to own stocks. In addition to higher fees, lower diversification and suboptimal risk-adjusted returns (even before fees), they are notably tax-inefficient.

Thankfully, the most onerous mutual fund fees, such as front-end load fees when you buy and termination fees when you sell, are not prevalent any more. But 12b-1 fees to cover the fund's own marketing and distributions costs, can be 25 to 75 basis points each year. Almost 70% of mutual funds charge 12b-1 fees while ETFs have no such charges. It is one of the reasons that mutual fund expense ratios are so high.

In addition, they generate a large amount of short-term and long-term capital gains from *within* the funds, which are passed on directly to your tax return and over which you have no control regarding the timing or holding period.

For instance, if the fund purchased $1,000 of Apple, it went up 25% in six months, and then the fund sold the stock, that would generate a $250 short-term gain passed directly to the fundholder. For a high-income taxpayer in a high-tax state, that would cost $125 in taxes, reducing the after-tax gain from 25% to 12.5%.

If instead, you owned Apple outright, you could (1) hold the stock until it was long-term, (2) defer the gain until a future tax year, (3) offset the gain with capital losses, (4) transfer the gain to a family member with a lower tax rate or (5) donate the stock to charity and permanently eliminate the taxable gain.

Part of the problem is that mutual funds must distribute gains and losses incurred *within* the fund, whereas ETFs do not because they have different tax rules. The other part is that mutual funds have high "turnover." Turnover is the ratio of the assets sold during a tax year divided by the average value of the assets during the year. A fund that bought and sold $100 million of stock in a year when they had average assets of $100 million, has a turnover ratio of 1.0.

The average turnover of mutual funds is 0.6 to 0.7 – versus half that for ETFs – which means they are trading frequently. For a number of reasons, they trade for non-tax purposes and consider only pre-tax returns.

- Fund managers try to beat the market through stock picking and market timing

- Fund companies try to justify their fees by appearing busy on your behalf
- Firms engage in "window dressing" towards the end of each quarter by buying recently-hot stocks and selling losers to look better in the quarterly reports.

This generates capital gains – predominantly short-term capital gain – that cannot be timed and managed for the fundholders. Fund managers are more concerned about their fund's pre-tax portfolios looking good than their customer's after-tax portfolios doing well. That is not unexpected, because that is how they are compensated.

In addition to the disadvantages of most mutual funds generally, three types of mutual funds have special investment and/or tax disadvantages.

- "Balanced" funds contain a mix of stocks and bonds. This makes the asset location – the tax strategy of putting the right assets in the right accounts – impossible.

- "Target date" funds are balanced funds built for people of a specific age. They automatically change the stock/bond ratio as you get older. This means that everyone your age gets exactly the same portfolio every year until you die. But not all 50-year-olds are the same and not all 50-year-olds want or should have the same portfolio.

- "Tax-managed" funds, which attempt lower turnover and tax loss harvesting within the fund itself, are the right concept but the wrong implementation. This can be done much more effectively with individual stocks.

Municipal Bonds Fund Local Infrastructure Projects

Munis are exempt from federal taxes, and "triple tax free" munis are also exempt from state and local taxes.

Municipal Bonds

Munis (pronounced myoo•neez) are mid-term and long-term bonds issued by towns, cities, counties and states to fund general obligations and to finance capital projects, such as building roads, schools or sewer systems.

> *"Municipal bonds – especially triple tax free munis – are a tax bonanza."*

Municipal bonds – especially triple tax free munis – are a tax bonanza. They are exempt from all federal taxes, including the NIIT. In the following cases, they do not incur state and local taxes as well.

1. Municipal bonds issued by the jurisdiction in which the bond holder resides are generally exempt from state and local taxes – these are known as triple tax

free munis. (States that may tax residents on some in-state municipal bond interest include Oklahoma, Illinois, Iowa and Wisconsin.)Seven states have no state income tax.

2. Municipal bonds issued by Puerto Rico are exempt from state and local tax in all 50 states and the District of Columbia.
3. Some states do not have a state income tax.

Triple tax free bonds are particularly valuable in areas with high state and local taxes. Partly as a result, California and New York issue one third of all the munis in the country.

To compare the after-tax yield of different types of bonds, look at the "tax-equivalent yield." This equals the pre-tax yield a taxable bond would have to generate to provide the same after-tax return as a taxable bond.

However, the yields on municipal bonds are significantly lower than rates on Treasury and corporate bonds, so they are a good option only for investors with high marginal tax rates.

Bonds with the highest credit ratings (AAA or AA+) are paying these very approximate rates. The tax-equivalent yields are shown for the highest-bracket residents of California (54.1% top tax rate) and Texas (40.8% top tax rate).

	Pre-Tax Yield	Tax-Equivalent Yield	
		California	Texas
Corporate Bonds	4.6%	4.6%	4.6%
Treasury Bonds	4.4%	5.1%	4.4%
Municipal Bonds	2.9%	4.9%	4.9%
Triple Tax Free Munis	2.9%	6.3%	4.9%

There are some additional considerations with munis:

- Munis have a slightly greater risk of default than a Treasury bond, depending on the issuer and type.
  - General obligation bonds are backed by the general funds of the municipality itself.
  - Revenue bonds are secured by the revenue from a specific project such as a toll road and therefore have a greater risk of default.

- Munis have long maturities of five years or more and have lower liquidity, so they are not an ideal place to hold short-term cash.

- There are many different munis of different types from different municipalities with different yields, so you need a professional to select appropriate bonds.

- As a result, most investors use municipal bond ETFs and mutual funds which carry annual expense ratios between 0.2% and 0.5%.

- Municipal bond funds and ETFs do not require manual reporting of the tax-exempt income that is required for Treasury bond funds and ETFs, because the interest is automatically reported on box 8 of the 1099-INT you receive from your broker.

"Triple tax free munis are a screaming deal – they are 100% tax free."

Triple tax free municipal bonds do not incur federal, state or local taxes when held by a resident of the issuing jurisdiction. For high-income residents of high-tax states, triple tax free munis are a screaming deal – they are 100% tax free.

Guaranteed by the US

Treasury securities and the obligations of federal agencies are exempt from state and local income taxes.

Treasury Bonds

Treasury bonds and bills are the opposite of municipal bonds – they are exempt from all state and local taxes but are *not* exempt from federal tax.

So, they are particularly valuable in high-tax states with maximum state and local tax rates of 10% or more, such as California, New York, New Jersey, Oregon, Minnesota, Hawaii and the District of Columbia.

Here are the marginal tax rates and brackets for single filers with taxable income of $200,000, $250,000 and $1,000,000. Four cities with high city surcharges are included as well.

$200k Income Single Taxpayer	Tax Rate	$250k Income Single Taxpayer	Tax Rate	$1,000k Income Single Taxpayer	Tax Rate
OR - Portland	12.40%	OR - Portland	13.90%	OR - Portland	13.90%
Hawaii	11.00%	Hawaii	11.00%	NY - New York City	13.53%
Oregon	9.90%	NY - New York City	10.73%	California	13.30%
NY - New York City	9.88%	Oregon	9.90%	Hawaii	11.00%
Minnesota	9.85%	Minnesota	9.85%	District of Columbia	10.75%
California	9.30%	California	9.30%	New Jersey	10.75%
MD - Baltimore	8.70%	District of Columbia	9.25%	Oregon	9.90%
District of Columbia	8.50%	MD - Baltimore	8.95%	Minnesota	9.85%
Vermont	7.60%	Vermont	8.75%	New York (>$1,077k)	9.65%
Maine	7.15%	Maine	7.15%	Massachusetts	9.00%
Washington (cap gain)	7.00%	Washington (cap gain)	7.00%	MD - Baltimore	8.95%
PA - Philadelphia	6.94%	PA - Philadelphia	6.94%	Vermont	8.75%
Montana	6.75%	Connecticut	6.90%	Wisconsin	7.65%
Nebraska	6.64%	New York	6.85%	Maine	7.15%
Delaware	6.60%	Montana	6.75%	Washington (cap gain)	7.00%
South Carolina	6.50%	Nebraska	6.64%	Connecticut	6.99%
Connecticut	6.50%	Delaware	6.60%	PA - Philadelphia	6.94%
New Jersey	6.37%	South Carolina	6.50%	Montana	6.75%
New York	6.00%	New Jersey	6.37%	Nebraska	6.64%

For a single filer with taxable income of $250,000 in Portland, a Treasury security with a 5.2% pre-tax yield would provide a 6.0% tax equivalent yield.

Although the credit agencies took the credit rating of US Treasuries down a notch during the debt ceiling crisis of 2023, they are generally considered the safest bonds in the world.

Treasuries are "guaranteed by the full faith and credit of the United States." Bank accounts and CDs are obligations of the bank, not of the federal government. FDIC insurance is only a backstop and only up to $250,000 per depositor per bank. (There are interbank networks that allow you to automatically spread your money across multiple banks and increase those limits.)

Treasury bonds are issued as four types: (1) Treasury bills with four-week, eight-week, 13-week, 27-week and 52-week maturities, (2) Treasury notes with maturities of two to ten years (3) Treasury bonds with maturities of up to 30 years and (4) Treasury Inflation-Protected Securities (TIPS).

Treasury notes and bonds have very small default risk, but they do have interest rate risk. The longer the remaining duration of the bond, the greater the interest rate risk, because the price of bonds goes up when interest rates go down and up when interest rates go up. So the market value of longer-term Treasury bonds are more volatile and fluctuate with interest rates.

"Treasury bills are the safest of all."

Treasury *bills* are the safest of all. Because of their government guarantee they have very low default risk and because of the short durations they have very low interest risk. In academic circles, the yield on the shortest term T-bills is often referred to as the "risk-free rate."

Treasury Inflation-Protected Securities (TIPS) are unique and offer protection when inflation is high or risking. They are issued only in longer terms (five-year, 10-year and 30-year maturities), so they carry interest rate risk. But that risk is partially offset by an automatic inflation adjustment. They offer protection against inflation for people on a fixed income, but their interest rates are lower than the rates on other Treasury bonds.

Here's how they work. The interest rate on the bond is fixed, but the principal is increased each year by the increase in the Consumer Price Index (CPI). Interest is then earned on the new principal amount. As a tax bonus, changes in the principal amount are treated as capital gains rather than ordinary income like the interest payments are.

Corporate Bonds Have the Highest Tax Rates

But investors pay tax at ordinary income rates, up to 54.7% if you live in Portland, Oregon.

Corporate Bonds

Corporate bonds are debt obligations of individual corporations and corporate bond funds and ETFs are pooled collections of many different corporate bonds. For most investors, owning a number of individual bonds is too cumbersome. Choose bond ETFs over bond funds because they are generally less expensive and more diversified.

The biggest differentiator between bonds is the credit rating which, from best to worst, is AAA, AA, A, BBB, BB, B, CCC, CC, C, or D. (There is no F, although perhaps that should mean "failed.") Bonds rated BB or lower carry high default risk and are referred to as "non-investment grade," "high yield" or "junk" bonds.

> *"Corporate bonds are tied to the yields on Treasury bonds plus spread."*

The yields on corporate bonds are tied to the yields on Treasury bonds plus a risk-based "spread." The spread on high-grade corporate bonds is typically 1.0% to 1.5% and the spread on high-yield bonds is typically 3.0% to 5.0%. For example, if the Treasury bond yield was 5.0%, a similar high-grade corporate bond would yield 6.0% to 6.5%.

Interest payments, or "coupon" payments, are typically made twice a year and taxed at ordinary income rates. Unlike municipal or Treasury bonds, they are not exempt from any federal, state or local taxes.

If a bond is purchased at original issuance and held to maturity, all of the return is interest. If it is purchased on the secondary market after issuance and/or sold prior to maturity, it will likely be purchased and/or sold at prices above or below the face value of the bond. In this case, in addition to the interest payments, the holder will have capital gain or loss equal to the sale price minus the purchase price.

Longer-term bonds are more likely to generate larger capital gains and losses, because the market value of bonds go down when interest rates fall and go up when interest rates rise. The longer the term of the bond, the greater the change in market value.

This creates an interesting tax wrinkle. If you purchase a bond at a price below the face value, the interest payments will be less than the total yield and the rest will be converted into capital gain which is taxed at a lower rate and for which the timing of recognition of the gain can be controlled. However, if you purchase a bond at a price above the face value, you will recognize interest income in excess of the total yield, offset by a capital loss. This is disadvantageous because it increases tax rate and accelerates the recognition of the total yield of the bond.

> *"Zero coupon bonds, like Treasury bills, do not make interest payments."*

Zero-coupon bonds, like Treasury bills, do not make interest payments. Instead, the bonds are sold at a discount to the value at maturity. The yield is the amount of the discount divided by the amount of time until maturity. Although this sounds like it would be capital gain, the IRS treats it as imputed interest and taxes it in each tax year at ordinary income rates.

Interest Rates at Large Banks are Microscopic

Chase bank has 4,700 branches and needs low-cost deposits to pay for all the people and real estate.

CDs and Savings Accounts

For investors with high marginal total tax rates, CDs and savings accounts are one of the least attractive places to store money you don't need for immediate uses. They are fully taxable at federal, state and local levels.

For a California resident at the top tax rate, a CD with a 4.0% advertised yield produces a 1.8% after-tax yield, and for a similar resident of Texas the after-tax yield is 2.4%. After inflation, you are losing purchasing power.

CDs also tie up your money for the duration of the CD, which is typically one year or more. If you need the money sooner, you will be charged an early withdrawal penalty that can range up to one year's interest or, in some cases, up to 3% of the amount withdrawn.

Online high-yield savings accounts pay high interest but, in addition to being subject to ordinary income tax rates, they are cumbersome to use. If you have a checking account at a large bank, you need to manually transfer money back and forth between the banks to maintain checking balances that are neither too low nor too high.

It's easier to use a savings account at the same large bank, but the interest rates are embarrassingly low – often less than a quarter of a percent. Big banks get away with this because they know it's painful to manually move your money in and out of the bank. These low rates, as well as overdraft fees, swell the profits of the banks by tens of billions of dollars each year.

Because bank interest rates are so low, the taxes are tiny as well. In that sense, it is an effective tax reduction strategy, but one to avoid.

"Bitcoin is the greatest financial scam in history"

When I said this in 2018, I was wrong. Other crypto scams have emerged that are bigger than Bitcoin and more fraudulent.

Cryptocurrency

I have been speaking out against cryptocurrency for over ten years. During that time, I have often been wrong about the temporal market value, but I am not wrong about the ultimate value of crypto.

Cryptocurrency has no utility. There is nothing you can do with crypto that cannot be done better and safer with dollars, euros, yen or pounds. (Except, of course, for criminal activity.)

It is not practical as a means of payment and, after 14 years, is still rarely used for that purpose. As a payment method, it is slow, expensive, cumbersome, not scalable and not widely accepted.

As a store of value, proponents claim it is immune from government-caused inflation and can function as a stable repository "just like gold." This is preposterous. Goldbugs are not always correct about the price stability of gold, but the wild price volatility of crypto renders it absurd as a safe haven for your money.

Proponents claim that crypto is highly secure, because it creates an "immutable public record of all transactions." But I am unaware of a single instance of financial fraud perpetrated by malicious alteration of bank databases.

The rampant sources of consumer fraud are phishing, account takeover and other forms of identity theft. In this regard, cryptocurrency is a huge step backwards. Just as the financial industry is completing its transformation to biometric and multi-factor authentication, crypto is taking us back to the bad old days of passwords, in the form of a string of numbers called your "private key." If you lose your key, or someone copies it, your money is gone forever with no avenue for recovery.

Crypto should be outlawed on the grounds of climate change alone. Bitcoin – just one of more than 1,000 coins in circulation – consumes more electricity each year than the country of Argentina.

 Cryptocurrency is a con game where people try to convince you that nothing is something. As a result, it attracts a raft of promoters and fraudsters. Each year there is another round of spectacular scandals and failures, and each year the crypto community says the most recent round is the last. It turns out that financial regulation is a good thing.

The messianic visions are absurd. A number of years ago, one of the more respectable crypto promoters proclaimed, "Bitcoin is bigger than the internet, bigger than the Iron Age, bigger than the Renaissance – it's bigger than the Industrial Revolution." Don't miss the fact that, throughout the history of crypto, most of the profits went to promoters and most of the losses went to customers.

> *"Cryptocurrency is the messiest asset you can own."*

The tax when using regular currencies is simple – there is none. The tax when using cryptocurrency is maddeningly complex. It is the messiest asset you can own.

- People who own crypto tend to trade it frequently, meaning that most of the winnings are short-term capital gains at ordinary income rates.

- Because of frequent trading, it's difficult to defer, transfer or eliminate the capital gains.

- There is a new tax event every time you sell, transfer or pay for something with coins, and there is a tax event every time you trade one coin for another, like Bitcoin for Ethereum.

- Record-keeping is difficult and many exchanges do not provide tax statements. This means hours or weekends laboring over spreadsheets of your own – particularly if you trade in more than one coin.

- If you make payments or small transfers, record-keeping is next to impossible. Every single movement of every sliver of a coin is a taxable event.

- Add to that the proliferation of tax lots. Every time you buy crypto you create another tax lot and every time you sell crypto you need to match that sale with the cost basis of prior tax lots using FIFO, LIFO, average cost or specific lot methods. (I'm not even going to try to explain these methods here.)

"If you lose your private key you lose your crypto."

- If you lose your private key and therefore lose your investment, how can you prove it to the IRS?

How do crypto holders handle the tax reporting burdens? Many simply don't report, or they only report the large purchases and sales. Even worse, some holders report their losses and not their gains.

I am an advocate of legal tax minimization. I am not an advocate of illegal tax evasion. Don't buy crypto.

Tax **Deductions**

Tax deductions lower your taxable income, reducing marginal tax rates as well as taxes due

Tax deductions reduce your taxable income, so a $1,000 deduction is worth $1,000 times your marginal tax rate, or $400 at a 40% marginal tax rate. Tax credits reduce your taxes due on a dollar-for-dollar basis, so a $1,000 credit is worth $1,000. Everyone has at least one tax deduction – the standard deduction – but tax credits are specialized and infrequent.

The large majority of taxpayers take the standard deduction because it is simpler and more favorable unless you have large unreimbursed medical expenses, mortgage interest or charitable contributions.

Here are the key concepts to understand tax deductions.

	Total income
minus	Above-the-line deductions
equals	Adjusted Gross Income (AGI)
minus	Standard deduction or itemized deductions
equals	Taxable income

- **Total Income.** Your income from all sources, including earned income, interest, dividends and capital gains, even though they carry different tax rates. Business income is reduced by related business expenses.

- **Above-the-line deductions.** Specific expenses that are deducted from your total income before calculating Adjusted Gross Income.

- **Adjusted Gross Income (AGI).** Your total income minus above-the-line deductions.

- **Standard deduction.** A predetermined amount based on your age and filing status, which can be used *instead* of itemizing deductions.

- **Itemized deductions.** Specific expenses such as charitable donations that are subtracted from AGI, if you use them *instead* of the standard deduction.

- **Taxable income.** AGI minus either the standard deduction or your itemized deductions.

- **Modified Adjusted Gross Income (MAGI).** Your AGI with certain deductions and exclusions added back, used to determine eligibility for various tax credits and benefits.

Above-the-line Deductions

The advantage of above-the-line deductions is that they can be claimed regardless of whether you take the standard deduction or itemize.

- Self-employment deductions: If you run your own business, you can deduct expenses such as half of your self-employment tax, self-employed retirement plans, and health insurance premiums.

- Student loan deductions: For those grappling with student loan debt, there's some relief. You can deduct the interest paid on student loans up to $2,500.

- HSA deductions: Contributions to Health Savings Accounts are deductible. The annual contribution limit for an HSA for individual coverage is $3,850 in 2023, and for families the limit is $7,750.

- Retirement account deductions: Contributions to certain retirement accounts — like traditional IRA and 401k accounts — can be deducted, which can directly lower your adjusted gross income.

Other above-the-line deductions include educator expenses, certain business expenses, moving expenses for Armed Forces members, penalties on early-withdrawal of savings, and alimony payments from a pre-2019 divorce.

Above-the-line deductions are subject to modified adjusted gross income (MAGI) phase-outs. IRS-defined thresholds gradually reduce or eliminate contribution deductibility based on income. Each retirement account has specific MAGI phase-out ranges, which change annually and depend on filing status and employer retirement plans. As MAGI rises, deduction amounts decrease and phase out at higher income levels.

Standard Deduction vs Itemized Deductions

Once you have calculated your adjusted gross income by subtracting above-the-line deductions from your total income, the next step is to determine whether you are better off itemizing your below-the-line deductions or simply taking the standard deduction. The IRS lets you choose either method.

Most people — 87.3% of all filers in 2020, according to the IRS — take the standard deduction. However, taxpayers with higher income and wealth are much more likely to itemize.

The major reasons people would choose to itemize include significant medical expenses, state and local taxes, mortgage interest, and charitable contributions.

A good way to evaluate whether itemizing will reduce your tax bill is to use tax preparation software to make the calculation both ways after the end of the tax year. However, to be prepared to itemize, you should keep detailed records of eligible expenses throughout the year.

Standard Deduction

The standard deduction, a cornerstone of the U.S. tax system, has undergone significant changes and expansions since its inception in 1944. Initially introduced to simplify the tax filing process, it has evolved over the years, with a notable expansion under the Tax Cuts and Jobs Act of 2017.

The standard deduction is especially beneficial for taxpayers who don't have a significant amount of itemizable expenses or don't mind foregoing possible deductions in return for not having to keep detailed records of their deductible expenses.

The standard deduction reduces your AGI resulting in lower taxable income, lower taxes and potentially a lower marginal tax rate. Some states also use a standard deduction for calculation of income tax.

The standard deduction for the 2024 tax year varies based on filing status.

- Single taxpayers: $14,600
- Married couples filing jointly: $29,299
- Married individuals filing separately: $14,600
- Heads of household: $21,900

For taxpayers over 65, an additional $1,950 is added to the standard deduction for single and head of household and an additional $1,550 per person is added for married filing jointly or separately.

Itemized Deductions

Compared to the standard deduction, itemized deductions are a more complex, but potentially more beneficial, approach to reducing taxable income. While the standard deduction is a flat amount, itemized deductions require taxpayers to list and calculate specific allowable expenses.

The major categories of itemized deductions include:

- Charitable contributions
- State and local taxes (SALT)
- Medical expenses
- Home mortgage interest

Each category has its own regulations and limitations.

Charitable Contributions

There are a few rules of thumb to keep in mind if you are looking to lower your AGI through charitable gifts.

The amount you can deduct for charitable contributions is generally limited to a percentage of your Adjusted Gross Income (AGI).

- Cash donations to public charities: 60% AGI
- Cash donations to private foundations: 30% AGI
- Non-cash gifts (like stocks) to public charities: 30% AGI
- Non-cash gifts to private foundations: 20% AGI

Charitable contribution deductions that exceed the AGI limits in a given year can be carried forward for up to five years.

Two common ways to donate to charity are direct giving and donor advised funds (DAFs):

- **Direct donations.** These are as simple as they sound. Pick a charity, make a donation, and claim the deduction in the same tax year. Just remember, for any donation over $250, the IRS requires a written acknowledgment from the charity.

- **Donor advised funds (DAFs).** If you like the idea of donating now but deciding on the beneficiaries later, DAFs are worth exploring. You get the tax deduction in the year you contribute to the DAF, with the freedom to allocate funds to specific charities over time. The tax deduction limits are the same as direct donations, and the DAF sponsor handles the administrative side of things.

Also, IRS rules require proper documentation for claiming charitable deductions. Here's what you need to know:

- **Receipts for large donations.** Get written acknowledgment from the charity for contributions of $250 or more.

- **Workplace donations.** Maintain pay stubs or payroll records for workplace contributions.

- **Non-cash contributions.** Document non-cash donations with descriptions, values, and how you determined them. Keep in mind, non-cash donations under $250 are generally not deductible.

- **Retention period.** Keep records for at least three years from your tax filing date.

State and Local Taxes

State and local tax (SALT) deductions typically include property taxes, state income taxes, and local income or sales taxes. These deductions allow you to reduce your federal tax liability by deducting certain taxes paid at the state and local level.

But there are limits regarding SALT deductions: They are currently capped $10,000 ($5,000 for married individuals filing separately). The TCJA affected taxpayers in high-tax states the most, as their state and local tax liabilities often surpass the threshold.

Before the Tax Cuts and Jobs Act of 2017 (TCJA), taxpayers could deduct an unlimited amount of state and local property taxes, as well as either state and local income taxes or sales taxes.

This arrangement was particularly beneficial to residents of high-tax states, where substantial state income and property taxes could be fully deducted from federal taxable income. For many, this deduction significantly lowered their federal tax liability.

There were three reasons behind the limitation of SALT deductions. First, it helped offset the cost of other tax cuts in the TCJA. Second, the unlimited SALT deduction effectively subsidized residents in states with high state and local taxes. Third, the TCJA was a Republican bill whereas high-tax states tend to be Democratic.

For many taxpayers, particularly in states with high state and local taxes, the cap has meant a noticeable increase in their federal tax bill.

Medical Expenses

You can deduct unreimbursed medical expenses that exceed 7.5% of your adjusted gross income (AGI).

For example, if your AGI is $150,000, you'll need to have unreimbursed medical expenses exceeding $11,250 (7.5% of $150,000) before you can start deducting.

The medical deduction includes a wide variety of expenses, including payments for diagnosis, cure, mitigation, treatment, or prevention of disease, and for treatments affecting any part or function of the body.

Here are the most commonly claimed deductible medical expenses:

- Hospital care
- Nursing home care if it is primarily for medical purposes
- Psychiatric and mental health care

- Transportation costs to get to medical appointments
- Payments to healthcare providers, including dentists, doctors, mental health professionals, and surgeons.
- Prescription drugs
- Prescription eyeglasses or contact lenses
- Hearing aids

Some commonly overlooked eligible costs include health insurance premiums, hospital stays, doctor appointments, prescriptions, and alternative treatments. You need to keep detailed records of all medical expenses, including bills and records from care providers. When filing your taxes, attach Schedule A to your Form 1040 to calculate and report the deduction.

Your state might have a lower AGI threshold for medical expense deductions, which could affect your deduction amount.

Home Loans

The home loan deduction allows you to deduct the interest you pay on your mortgages and certain home equity debts from your taxable income. This applies to interest you pay on your primary or secondary personal residences, not on rental or business properties (although this can be deducted from business income).

You can deduct mortgage interest every year plus any upfront points you paid when securing the mortgage. Although points are arguably prepaid interest, you can deduct them in the year you paid them.

Home equity loans and home equity lines of credit (HELOCs) also offer tax benefits under certain conditions. Interest on home equity debt is deductible if used to buy, build, or substantially improve your primary or secondary personal residence. However, it is not deductible if the proceeds are used for other purposes like debt consolidation or personal expenses.

The TCJA introduced lower limits on eligible mortgage and home equity debt. For debt incurred after December 15, 2017, the deduction is limited to interest paid on up to $750,000 of combined mortgage and home equity debt. Older mortgages maintain a limit of $1,000,000.

To claim this deduction, you need to maintain accurate records of home loan interest payments. Your lender will typically provide Form 1098, the Mortgage Interest Statement, outlining interest paid during the year.

Less Common Itemized Deductions

Other itemized deductions that could lower your taxable income and save taxes include:

Casualty and theft losses. Property losses due to natural disasters or criminal acts qualify for this deduction, if the loss exceeds 10% of your Adjusted Gross Income (AGI).

Military moving expenses. Military personnel can deduct moving expenses when they relocate due to military orders.

Gambling losses. You can deduct gambling losses, but only up to the amount of your winnings each year. If you win $2,000 and lose $1,000, your net gambling income is $1,000. But if you win $2,000 and lose $3,000, your net gambling income is zero, not a loss of $1,000.

Business losses. The 2017 Tax Cuts and Jobs Act limits the deduction of business losses for sole proprietorships and partnerships on personal tax returns to $250,000 for single filers or $500,000 for joint filers.

Tax-Advantaged **Accounts**

There are multiple tax benefits to tax advantaged accounts like a 401k, IRA or Roth account

If you're investing money — be it for retirement, your child's education, or healthcare needs — you can take advantage of various tax breaks. Uncle Sam wants you to invest for long-term goals, and the federal government offers tax breaks for two types of tax advantaged accounts:

- Tax-deferred accounts: You can delay paying taxes on the money you contribute to an employer 401k or an individual retirement account (IRA) until you take withdrawals.

- Tax-exempt accounts: If you contribute money after-taxes to a Roth 401k or a Roth IRA, then you won't owe taxes when you take out money in retirement.

Tax-advantaged accounts reduce your tax burden and allow your money to grow faster, which is why you should prioritize saving in these accounts versus others. The tax savings can be quite significant because you are only taxed on the money in these accounts once — either before you make contributions or when you take withdrawals.

Of course, you can always invest additional money in a taxable brokerage account. But you won't enjoy the same tax breaks. Contributions are made with after-tax dollars and investment income is taxed as it is received rather than compounding tax free.

> *"Many companies offer to match your contributions to a 401k plan."*

Tax savings are the most obvious benefit of tax advantaged accounts, though many companies offer a match on contributions to your employer-sponsored 401k plan, which is an additional perk. Deciding how to allocate your money between these accounts will depend on whether you have access to a workplace 401k plan, your income, your age and your investing goals.

When you are planning for retirement, you have some excellent options to choose from: traditional 401ks, Roth 401ks, traditional IRAs, Roth IRAs and other more specialized retirement accounts. With traditional 401ks and IRAs, you get a tax break upfront, but you'll pay taxes later when you withdraw. Roth options flip the script – you pay taxes now, but your retirement withdrawals are tax-free.

	Traditional 401k or IRA	Roth 401k or IRA	Taxable Accounts
Tax on withdrawals	Ordinary income tax	Tax-free	Capital gains tax

	(max 37%)		(max 20%)
Notes	Required minimum distributions (RMD)	No RMDs and no tax on distributions	Methods to defer or eliminate taxes

Employer 401k

A majority of private-sector employers offer a retirement savings plan to employees as part of a broader benefits package. The 401k plan is only for corporate employers, but there are also 403b plans for nonprofits, 457b plans for state and local governments and TSP plans for the federal government. These are "defined contribution" plans and represent 70% of the retirement plan assets in private companies. Governments still have 90% of their retirement plan assets in "defined benefit" plans like pensions.

A 401k plan is a dedicated investment account for retirement savings. There are two types — traditional and Roth (more on those later) — and the difference comes down to when you're taxed. With a traditional 401k, you get an immediate tax break because contributions are tax-deductible, so you can lower your taxable income for the year.

Many employers offer a valuable incentive to contribute to your 401k: They match employee contributions up to a certain percentage of your salary, often about 3% to 5%. This free money makes funding a 401k worthwhile, at least up to the amount of the match — if not more.

How a traditional 401k works:

- You sign up through your employer, though some companies require you to work for a period of time before you become eligible to make contributions.
- Contributions are automatically deducted from your paycheck after you choose the percentage or dollar amount of your pre-tax salary to contribute.
- Contributions must be made by the end of the calendar year.
- You must make required minimum distributions starting at the age of 73.

Your annual contributions to a 401k are limited at $23,000, or $30,500 if you are over 50. The combined total contributions from you and your employer are limited at $69,000.

Benefits of a traditional 401k:

- Tax savings: Your contributions to a 401k are tax-deductible and reduce your taxable income for the year — and you defer paying taxes on contributions and earnings until you withdraw money from the account.

- Free money: If your employer offers matching contributions, this free money will help you save even more for retirement.

- Good for beginners: If you're new to investing, this is an easy way to get started, and many 401k plan administrators offer free tools that will help with your retirement planning.

- Convenience: It's easy and free to sign up for a plan through your employer — some companies auto-enroll new employees unless they opt out — and contributions are automatically deducted from your paycheck.

"If your employer offers matching contributions, this free money will help you save even more for retirement."

Downsides of a traditional 401k:

- Limited investment options: Many employer 401k plans offer a limited number of investment options, particularly when compared with a taxable brokerage account.

- Investment fees: Some 401k plans charge high investment management and administrative fees.

- Eligibility restrictions: Some employers require new hires to work at the company for a specified period of time before becoming eligible for a plan — or to stay at the company for a certain number of years in order to be fully vested in the employer's match.

- Early withdrawal penalties: You'll generally be charged a 10% penalty if you withdraw money from your account before the age of 59½, though you may be able to take a distribution because of a hardship or take a loan from your account.

Tradeoffs of an employer 401k:

The tax benefits of a 401k can be substantial: Making contributions to your 401k means you reduce your taxable income now and defer paying taxes on contributions and earnings until you withdraw money from your account in retirement. Add in matching contributions from your employer, and it's a good idea to contribute at least enough money to max out this benefit.

If your employer offers a higher-than-average match on contributions and fees that are lower-than-average — you can find ratings for 401k plans online — you may want to consider maxing out your 401k contributions. You should also assess your financial situation and investing goals when deciding if that's the right move for you.

Individual Retirement Account (IRA)

An IRA is another type of tax-advantaged retirement-savings account that is not affiliated with your employer. These accounts are designed to help people save for retirement — either as a supplement to a 401k or in place of one.

Like a 401k, an IRA is a dedicated investment account for retirement savings with both traditional and Roth options.

Similarly, contributions are tax-deductible, so funding an IRA can help you reduce your taxable income for the year. Your contributions and earnings grow tax-deferred in the account, though you're taxed on withdrawals.

How a traditional IRA works:

- You must typically sign up for an IRA on your own, though some states have IRA plans for employees of small businesses.
- You will decide when and how much money you contribute to your IRA.
- You may be able to deduct some or all of your IRA contributions, depending on your income.
- You have until tax day in April to make IRA contributions for the prior tax year.

> *"You may be able to deduct some or all of your IRA contributions."*

Your annual contributions to a traditional IRA are limited at $7,000, or $8,000 if you are over 50. However, if you are covered by a workplace plan such as a 401k, the tax deductibility of your contributions is fully phased out if your taxable income (AGI) exceeds:

- $87,000 if you are single or head of household
- $143,000 if you are married filing jointly
- No phaseout if neither spouse is covered by a workplace plan.

Benefits of a traditional IRA:

- More investment options: You can choose from a broader array of investments in an IRA — including individual stocks — and you can actively trade in this account, if you so choose.

- Defer taxes: You defer all investing-related taxes on money in a traditional IRA until you begin taking withdrawals — this means you can actively buy and sell investments in your IRA and you won't have to pay capital gains taxes on your profits or investment income.

- Flexibility and portability: Because an IRA isn't tied to your employment, you can decide where to open your account, when you want to make contributions, and you can easily move the account to another company.

- Tax savings: Anyone can contribute the full amount to an IRA, though you can only deduct contributions in part or in full if you meet specific criteria — you and your spouse don't have access to a workplace retirement plan, for example, or your income falls below specific thresholds depending on your filing status.

- Additional retirement savings: An IRA offers another tax-advantaged way to save for retirement, and can be especially valuable for people who don't have access to an employer 401k or want to save more money than is allowed in those accounts.

Downsides of a traditional IRA:

- Lower contribution limits: The annual contribution limits for an IRA are significantly lower than an employer 401k, and this amount may not sufficiently cover your retirement-savings needs.

- More decisions required: Whereas many decisions are made for you with an employer 401k — what company administers the plan, for example, and the investing options you can choose from — you'll be in the driver's seat for those decisions when funding an IRA.

- Early withdrawal penalties: As with a 401k, you'll generally be charged a 10% penalty if you withdraw money from your account before the age of 59½, though you may be able to take a hardship withdrawal from your account (loans, however, aren't allowed).

- Required minimum distributions: You must take mandatory withdrawals from your IRA starting at the age of 73 — or face a 25% penalty for failing to do so.

Tradeoffs of a traditional IRA:

The biggest advantage of a traditional IRA is you can grow your retirement savings on a tax-deferred basis and you won't have to pay any taxes until you begin taking withdrawals. You may be able to deduct some or all of your contributions, though it depends on your income, filing status, and whether you have a workplace retirement plan.

Even with lower contribution limits and required minimum distributions, an IRA offers a tax-advantaged way to save for retirement. Deciding whether to max out IRA contributions depends on your financial situation and investing goals, and you'll have until tax day of the following year to make contributions.

Roth 401k

If your company offers a 401k, odds are they also offer a Roth option. The difference between these types of accounts is when you're taxed: With a Roth 401k, you make contributions with after-tax dollars and then withdrawals are made tax-free.

While you won't get any immediate tax benefit in the form of deductions with a Roth 401k, the future tax savings could be significant. That's particularly true if you expect your tax rate will go up over time — and be higher in retirement than it is currently.

As with a traditional 401k, your employer may offer a match on contributions up to a certain percentage of your salary. Not all 401k plan administrators allow matching contributions to be added directly to a Roth 401, and some may require these funds be added to a traditional 401k.

A Roth 401k works the same as a traditional 401k, except:

- Contributions are automatically deducted from your paycheck with after-tax dollars.
- You are no longer required to take minimum distributions from a Roth 401k.
- You can withdraw contributions from your Roth 401k penalty-free at any time, though doing so generally isn't advisable.
- You can make withdrawals of contributions and earnings from a Roth 401k after the age of 59½, so long as your first contribution to the account was at least five years ago.
- The contribution limits for a Roth 401k are the same as a traditional 401k — and you can split contributions between both account types.

The benefits of a Roth 401k are similar to a traditional 401k with some exceptions:

- Tax-free withdrawals: You take the tax hit immediately with a Roth 401k by contributing with after-tax dollars, but the tradeoff is that you can make withdrawals tax-free — and you won't have to pay any taxes in the interim.

- No required minimum distribution: Unlike with a traditional 401k, you don't have to take required minimum distributions from your Roth account in retirement.

- Withdrawals could be more valuable in retirement: If tax rates go up with time — or if you're in a higher tax bracket in retirement — then withdrawals from a Roth 401k could be worth more because you can tap this money tax-free.

Many of the same downsides of a traditional 401k apply to a Roth 401k:

- Tax rate forecasting: Deciding whether a Roth 401k is preferable to a traditional 401k requires you to make a bet on what your tax rate will be in the future — if you expect your tax rate to go down in retirement, it may make more sense to contribute to a traditional 401k.

- Early withdrawal penalties: You'll generally be charged a 10% penalty if you withdraw money from your account before the age of 59½, though you may be able to take a distribution because of a hardship or take a loan from your account.

- Five-year rule for qualified withdrawals: Qualified withdrawals from a Roth 401k come with another restriction that doesn't apply to a traditional 401k — you must be at least 59½ years old and you also must have been contributing to the account for at least the five previous years.

Tradeoffs of a Roth 401k:

The tax benefits of a Roth 401k could potentially be even more substantial than a traditional 401k, though investing in this type of account means you're inherently making a bet on your future tax rates. If you expect your ordinary tax rate to be higher in retirement, a Roth 401k makes more sense than if you expect your tax rate to be lower.

The ability to make withdrawals tax-free in retirement is noteworthy for another reason: A vast majority of the money you will be withdrawing is appreciated returns on your investments — meaning that the value of your account will most likely be much larger than the amount of contributions you made.

The IRS recently eliminated required minimum distributions for a Roth 401k, which can make it easier to pass this money along to heirs. But the five-year rule related to qualified withdrawals may make a Roth 401k less appealing if you plan to tap your retirement savings early.

Finally, if your employer offers both a traditional and a Roth 401k, you may choose to split funds between the two account types, while still making the same considerations about whether maxing out contributions makes sense given your financial situation and the plan offerings.

Roth IRA

As with a Roth 401k, a Roth IRA allows you to make contributions with after-tax dollars and then take withdrawals tax-free. But a Roth IRA differs from a traditional IRA in one very important way: Your eligibility to fund a Roth IRA depends on your modified adjusted gross income (MAGI).

The amount of money you can contribute to a Roth IRA — or whether you can contribute any money at all — depends on income limits established by the IRS. That means a Roth IRA isn't an option if you're a high earner (though a Roth 401k is).

Roth IRAs also have more flexible withdrawal rules than a traditional IRA, there are fewer restrictions for withdrawals, and you can pass the money in this account tax-free to your heirs.

A Roth IRA works the same as a traditional IRA, except:

- Eligibility to contribute to a Roth IRA phases out at higher incomes.

- You are not required to take minimum distributions from a Roth IRA.

- You can withdraw contributions from your Roth IRA penalty-free at any time, though doing so generally isn't advisable.

Your annual contributions to a Roth IRA are limited at $7,000, or $8,000 if you are over 50. However, if you are covered by a workplace plan such as a 401k, the tax deductibility of your contributions is fully phased out if your taxable income (AGI) exceeds:

- $161,000 if you are single or head of household

- $240,000 if you are married filing jointly
- No phaseout if neither spouse is covered by a workplace plan.

The benefits of a Roth IRA are similar to a traditional IRA with some exceptions:

- Tax-free withdrawals: You take the tax hit immediately with a Roth IRA by contributing with after-tax dollars, but the tradeoff is you can take withdrawals tax-free — and you won't have to pay any taxes in the interim.

- No required minimum distribution: Unlike with a traditional IRA, you don't have to take required minimum distributions from your Roth IRA in retirement — and this makes it easier to transfer this money to heirs.

"You don't have to take required minimum distributions from your Roth IRA."

- Ability to tap contributions at any time: You can tap the contributions (but not the earnings) in your account early without taking a penalty since you've already paid taxes on these contributions — though it's generally advisable to avoid doing so.

Many of the same downsides of a traditional IRA apply to a Roth IRA, as well as:

- Eligibility limited by income: Whereas anyone can contribute to a traditional IRA, a Roth IRA is only available to taxpayers who meet specific income qualifications.

- Tax rate forecasting: As with the decision about a 401k plan, you must consider your potential future tax rate when weighing a Roth IRA versus a traditional option.

- Required minimum distribution for inherited Roth IRAs: You don't have to take required minimum distributions from a Roth IRA, but your beneficiaries must generally withdraw all the cash from the account within 10 years of your death (though there are exceptions, depending on the beneficiary).

- Five-year rule for qualified withdrawals from inherited IRAs: Roth IRA beneficiaries can withdraw contributions tax-free at any time, but they must pay taxes on earnings if the account was less than five years old when the original owner died.

Tradeoffs of a Roth IRA:

A Roth IRA could potentially offer more significant tax benefits than a traditional IRA because you can take withdrawals tax-free in retirement. But you must meet specific income requirements to be eligible to make contributions to a Roth IRA.

If you don't want to be subjected to minimum required distributions, a Roth IRA may be preferential to a traditional IRA, though it's important to note that your beneficiaries will need to withdraw money from an inherited Roth IRA within a specific timeframe. The ability to tap your contributions early, if needed, may also make a Roth IRA more appealing though the same type of five-year rule applies to qualified withdrawals as it does for a Roth 401k.

Finally, it's worth noting that over the course of your lifetime you may fund both a Roth and a traditional IRA, depending on your income at the time, and doing could help diversify your tax obligations.

> *"You won't find the term 'backdoor' mentioned by the IRS, but this conversion is completely legal."*

Backdoor Roth IRA

You can take advantage of the tax-free withdrawals of a Roth IRA even if you didn't qualify to contribute to this type of account because of your income. High earners may convert a traditional IRA to a Roth IRA with a strategy known as a backdoor Roth IRA. You won't find the term "backdoor" mentioned by the IRS, but this conversion is completely legal.

Converting a traditional IRA to a Roth IRA is a taxable event, however, so it's important to brace yourself for taxes when you do a backdoor conversion. The tradeoff is that the taxes you pay now will allow you to make tax-free withdrawals in retirement.

A step-by-step guide to a backdoor Roth IRA:

1. You must first make a non-deductible contribution to a traditional IRA account.
2. If you don't already have a Roth IRA, you'll need to open an account and then the company that administers your IRA will provide the necessary paperwork to help you with the conversion process.
3. Convert some or all of the funds in your traditional IRA to your Roth IRA.
4. Pay taxes on any untaxed amounts in the traditional IRA (this includes pre-tax IRA funds or earnings on your contributions).

A backdoor Roth IRA allows high earners to become eligible for a Roth IRA via a back door. The contribution limits for IRAs still stand, and it's important to be mindful of any potential tax implications related to this type of conversion.

Benefits of a backdoor Roth IRA:

- Expands Roth IRA eligibility: High-income earners don't qualify to make contributions to a Roth IRA because of income restrictions, though they can contribute to a Roth IRA with a backdoor conversion.

- Change tax implications: A backdoor conversion allows people to benefit from tax-free withdrawals, which is an appealing aspect of a Roth IRA in the first place.

- Flexibility: You can convert some or all of the money in your traditional IRA to a Roth IRA — and that decision is completely up to you, though you may want to assess the potential tax burden of converting earnings and other untaxed portions of these accounts.

Downsides of a backdoor Roth IRA:

- Process can be complicated: The steps required to convert a traditional IRA to a Roth IRA aren't so complex, but it's important to understand the potential tax implications — and this is why many people consult with a financial advisor for this type of account conversion.

- Tax bill: You will owe income taxes on any earnings in the traditional IRA at the time of conversion — and the portion of your traditional IRA that includes pre-tax dollars will be taxed pro-rata (meaning proportionally to your conversion).

- Other potential downsides of Roth IRAs apply: If you don't currently have a Roth IRA, you should be sure to review some of the other potential downsides of these accounts, including required minimum distributions for beneficiaries and the five-year rule for qualified withdrawals.

Tradeoffs of a backdoor Roth IRA:

The option to tap savings tax-free in retirement is enticing enough to many investors that they're willing to deal with the hassle and potential tax bill that comes with converting funds from a traditional IRA to a Roth IRA. That said, because these conversions can be a bit tricky, it's best to consult with a financial advisor first.

Retirement Account Withdrawals

Over time, the money you have invested in tax advantaged accounts will have grown and compounded tax free for decades.

If you withdraw funds from a traditional 401k or IRA (or a Roth 401k) before you are 59½, you must pay an early-withdrawal penalty of 10% of the amount of the withdrawal, plus applicable federal and state taxes. In a *Roth IRA* account, you can withdraw your original contributions (but not earnings) without an early-withdrawal penalty and you pay no federal or state tax on the withdrawals, because the contributions were made with after-tax dollars.

Distributions for certain purposes are not subject to the early withdrawal penalty, including:

- Some education tuition and other expenses
- Unreimbursed medical expenses that exceed 10% of your adjusted gross income for an IRA and 7.5% for a 401k
- Up to $10,000 for a first-time home purchase

- Rollovers to a new or different IRA where the distributions are reinvested within 60 days

In many 401k plans, you can also take a loan from your 401k account up to the lesser of $50,000 or one half your account balance for up to five years.

After age 59½, you may withdraw funds at any time without an early withdrawal penalty.

"As many as 20% of retirees run late taking required withdrawals – a very costly mistake."

During the year, as many as 20% of retirees run late taking required withdrawals – a very costly mistake. If not quickly rectified, this exposes you to a penalty equal to 25% of the required withdrawal.

However, the IRS requires that you start taking required minimum distributions (RMDs) from traditional IRA and 401k accounts after age 73. The required amount is based on a distribution factor that ranges from 27.4 to 1.9 and goes down the older you get. For instance, a 74-year-old with a $200,000 account balance as of the end of the prior year and a distribution factor of 25.5 would have a required distribution of $7,843.

$200,000 / 25.5 = $7,843

Failing to make required distributions is very punishing – the IRS imposes an additional **25% tax** on any shortfall. Shockingly, up to 20% percent of retirees are occasionally delinquent taking required withdrawals – a very costly mistake.

Roth IRA accounts do not have required distributions while the owner is still alive, however RMDs do apply to Roth 401k accounts until 2024. Be sure to convert Roth 401k accounts into Roth IRA accounts as soon as you stop working for the sponsoring employer.

RMD rules and requirements differ for the original owner, a surviving spouse, and someone who inherits the account upon the death of the original owner or spouse. If you have multiple retirement accounts, the RMDs must be separately calculated for and distributed from each account.

> *"There is no one-size-fits-all withdrawal strategy for every investor."*

There are three common withdrawal approaches:

- Conventional, where you withdraw from taxable accounts first, traditional retirement accounts second, and Roth retirement accounts last. This can be favorable when the value of tax-free compounding in your retirement accounts outweighs the capital gains tax on appreciated securities in your taxable account.

- Proportional, where you withdraw first from your taxable and traditional retirement accounts in proportion to their balances, and then from your Roth retirement accounts. This approach can help with RMDs.

- Personalized. Most taxpayers with significant assets are better served with custom-built withdrawal strategies.

Distributions from retirement accounts must be considered in conjunction with other retirement and estate planning objectives, so there is no one-size-fits-all withdrawal strategy for every investor.

RMDs and other withdrawal considerations can be mind-bendingly complicated, so you should seek guidance from a financial advisor or from the financial institution holding the account.

Health Savings Account

A Health Savings Account (HSA) is a tax advantaged account that lets you save specifically to pay for qualified medical expenses. You are only eligible to open an HSA if you have a high-deductible health insurance plan, but it's not tied to your employment. Many employers do offer the option of an HSA, but you can also open one on your own.

An HSA is an investment account, meaning you can buy stocks, bonds, mutual funds and ETFs. The funds are specifically earmarked to pay for medical expenses, and you can roll over unused funds each year to pay for future medical expenses.

How a Health Savings Account works:

- You must be enrolled in a high-deductible health plan (HDHP) to be eligible to open an HSA, and you're still eligible to open one of these accounts if this benefit isn't offered by your employer.
- Contributions are made with pre-tax dollars, which reduces your taxable income.
- You can make withdrawals for qualified medical expenses tax-free.
- Money in the account is invested in financial assets and earnings compound tax-free.
- There are no rollover limits for unused funds.
- You have until tax day in April to make HSA contributions for the prior tax year.

2024 HSA contribution limits are $4,150 for self-only coverage, $8,300 for family coverage and an additional $1,000 catch-up contribution for those over 50.

Benefits of an HSA:

- Triple tax benefit: Your contributions to an HSA are tax-deductible and reduce your taxable income for the year, your money grows tax-free over time, and your withdrawals are also tax-free, as long as you use the money for qualified medical expenses.

- Investment options: Not all HSAs are alike, but many allow you to make the investment decisions and choose securities that historically provide higher returns than a traditional savings account.

- Free money: Though not as common as a 401k match, some employers will match contributions to your HSA.

- Unused funds roll over: Each year, any money that you do not use to pay for qualified medical expenses can be rolled over to the subsequent year.

- Retirement savings: HSA accounts are designed to help people save for healthcare costs, but after the age of 65 you can withdraw money for any reason, though you'll be taxed on those withdrawals.

Downsides of an HSA:

- Require an HDHP: You can open an HSA even if your employer doesn't offer this benefit, but you must be enrolled in a high-deductible health plan.

- Limited investment options: The investment options offered by some HSAs can be lacking versus a taxable account.

- Another account to manage: Even though HSAs offer tax-efficient benefits, you will need to manage another investment account.

- Account fees: Some HSA providers charge annual account fees

- Limited contributions: The contribution limits are relatively low and may not be sufficient to cover a major medical expense

- Taxes and penalties on non-medical withdrawals: If you withdraw money from an HSA for a non-qualified purpose, you will be taxed on the withdrawal and incur an additional 20% penalty, though that penalty goes away after age 65.

Tradeoffs of an HSA:

The triple tax benefit and ability to save for future healthcare costs make Health Savings Accounts advantageous for many people. But you must be enrolled in a high-deductible health plan, which is not always the best option for your healthcare needs.

An HSA offers protection against unexpected medical expenses. They can also be a source of additional retirement income because you can withdraw money penalty-free after the age of 65 for any reason, although the withdrawal is subject to federal and state taxes at ordinary income rates.

529 Plans

You can save for the future education expenses for a child with a tax-advantaged 529 plan account. Formally known as a qualified tuition program, these plans are designed to cover the education costs of a designated beneficiary.

Contributions to 529 plans are made with after-tax dollars, so they are not deductible at a federal level, however some states offer deductions or credits for contributions. The money in a 529 grows tax-free, and withdrawals for qualified education expenses are also tax-free.

Most 529 plans are sponsored by individual states and the plan specifics can vary widely by sponsor.

How a 529 Plan works:

- You must open a 529 account with either your state's qualified tuition program or a financial institution.
- You must designate a beneficiary for the account.
- You must select investments for the account.
- Withdrawals are tax-free if they're used for qualified. education expenses, but you may be charged taxes and penalties on non-qualified withdrawals.

- Maximum contribution limits vary by state.

Benefits of a 529 Plan:

- Tax savings: Although contributions to a 529 plan are made with after-tax dollars, the money grows tax-free over time, and withdrawals for qualified education expenses are tax-free.

- State tax benefits: Many states offer incentives to encourage parents to fund a 529 plan, including tax deductions and credits.

- Plan for education costs: By setting aside money in a 529 plan, you can help plan for your child's future education costs — as can other family members.

- Unused funds roll over: Any money in a 529 that's not used can be rolled over to cover future education expenses or can be passed to another beneficiary.

Downsides of a 529 Plan:

- Unpredictability of educational needs: Your child's educational journey may not mirror yours, so setting aside money for qualified education expenses may not make sense.

- Penalty for non-qualified withdrawals: Withdrawals for non-qualified expenses will be taxed and hit with a 10% penalty.

- Investment options: The 529 account holder can decide how money in a plan is invested, but the array of investment options is often limited.

- Another investment account to manage: These plans require some understanding about state 529 plans and some people don't want to manage yet another investment account.

- Account fees: Fees associated with 529 Plans vary widely, but could include enrollment, annual account maintenance, and management fees.

- Rules related to account owners: While the account owner and beneficiary can be one in the same, generally a parent is the account owner and the child is the beneficiary, and their interests may not align.

"You are making a gamble on what your child's future education path will look like."

Tradeoffs of a 529 Plan:

A 529 Plan offers parents and other family members a tax advantaged way to save for a child's future education expenses. However, you are making a gamble on what the child's educational path will be. If that changes and you subsequently withdraw the funds, the withdrawals will be subject to federal and state taxes *plus* the 10% penalty.

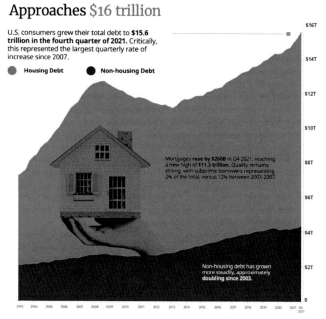

U.S. Consumer Debt
Approaches $16 trillion

U.S. consumers grew their total debt to **$15.6 trillion in the fourth quarter of 2021.** Critically, this represented the largest quarterly rate of increase since 2007.

● Housing Debt   ● Non-housing Debt

Mortgages **rose by $260B** in Q4 2021, reaching a new high of **$11.3 trillion.** Quality remains strong, with subprime borrowers representing 2% of the total, versus 12% between 2003-2007.

Non-housing debt has grown more steadily, approximately **doubling since 2003.**

$16T
$14T
$12T
$10T
$8T
$6T
$4T
$2T
0

2003 2004 2005 2006 2007 2008 2009 2010 2011 2012 2013 2014 2015 2016 2017 2018 2019 2020 2021 Q4 2021

Tax Advantaged **Credit**

The true after-tax cost of student, mortgage, home equity, margin, auto, personal, credit card and overdraft debt

If you need credit – whether it's credit card or mortgage debt – you need to know the true after-tax cost of your options.

There is more to consider than just the stated interest rate on the loan, especially the tax benefits of mortgage and home equity loans. From best to worst:

- **Student** debt has the lowest interest rates and is often tax deductible up to $2,500 if you itemize.

- **Mortgages** carry very low rates and are tax deductible, but don't forget the cost of points.

- **Home equity** loans have slightly higher rates than first mortgages and are usually tax deductible.

- **Margin** loans against your securities have low rates and are deductible if used to purchase more stocks.

- **Auto** loans are secured by your car, have lower rates than unsecured loans, but are not tax deductible.

- **Personal** unsecured loans are higher cost but can be less expensive than credit cards.

- **Credit card** revolving debt is easy to obtain and access, but is very high cost and not deductible.

- **Overdraft** on your checking account is absurdly expensive – don't do it!

In a 5% interest rate environment (using the federal funds rate at which banks borrow from the government), your after-tax interest rate can range from 3% to close-to-infinity. These estimates are very approximate and for illustration only.

Type of Debt	Pre-tax Interest Rate	After-tax Interest Rate
Student	5-8%	3-5%
Mortgage	7-9%	4-6%
Home Equity	8-10%	5-6%
Margin	9-12%	7-10%*
Auto	10-15%	10-15%
Personal	15-30%	15-30%
Credit Card	20-30%	20-30%
Overdraft	Infinity?	Infinity?

* Some margin loans are tax deductible.

When you need credit, you are playing a high-stakes zero-sum game against the banks.

"Your after-tax interest rate can range from 3% to close-to-infinity"

Which type of credit is right for you depends on your financial situation, tax rate, credit score, housing needs and other considerations.

Student Loans

To encourage pursuit of higher education, the federal government guarantees most student loans. They can be obtained directly from the government or from private lenders.

Because of this guarantee, student debt is the lowest cost credit available, and up to $2,500 of interest is tax deductible with phaseouts starting at $85,000 for singles and $165,000 for married filing jointly. Interest rates vary depending on whether the loan is taken by an undergraduate student, a graduate student or a parent.

Undergraduate students

- **5.50%** pre-tax interest rate for the 2023-2024 year
- **3.47%** after-tax interest rate for a taxpayer in the top federal tax bracket of 37% in a state with no tax
- **2.73%** after-tax interest rate if that same taxpayer also pays the top California tax rate of 13.3%

Graduate students

- **7.05%** pre-tax interest rate for the 2023-2024 year
- **4.44%** after-tax interest rate for a taxpayer in the top federal tax bracket of 37% in a state with no tax
- **3.50%** after-tax interest rate if that same taxpayer also pays the top California tax rate of 13.3%

Parents (Direct PLUS loan)

- **8.05%** pre-tax interest rate for the 2023-2024 year
- **5.07%** after-tax interest rate for a taxpayer in the top federal tax bracket of 37% in a state with no tax
- **4.00%** after-tax interest rate if that same taxpayer also pays the top California tax rate of 13.3%

Despite the low interest rates, student debt is a huge burden on a very large number of people in this country. 43 million Americans are paying interest on a total of $1.63 trillion of student debt. The debt is not concentrated among young adults.

- $500 billion held by people aged 25 to 34
- $632 billion held by people ages 35 to 49
- $296 billion held by people from 50 to 61
- $115 billion held by people 62 and older

A large part of this debt is held by parents financing college for their kids. Interest from student debt is tax deductible if it is for you, your spouse or dependents, such as your children.

"Student debt is tax deductible when used for you, your spouse or your dependents."

As much as it is satisfying to pay down student loans ahead of schedule, you're better off paying down other more expensive debt first.

Mortgages

Because they require a down payment and are secured by the house itself, mortgage loans carry very low pre-tax interest rates – assume 8% for a 30-year fixed loan in this 5% rate environment.

The interest on the first $750,000 of mortgage debt on your primary residence is tax deductible, which lowers the after-tax cost.

- **8.00%** pre-tax interest rate
- **5.04%** after-tax interest rate for a taxpayer in the top federal tax bracket of 37% in a state with no tax
- **3.98%** after-tax interest rate if that same taxpayer also pays the top California tax rate of 13.3%

If you own or are buying a house, this is the least costly type of debt. To claim the tax benefit, you must itemize deductions on your tax return rather than using the standard deduction.

Be careful of the "points" charged on the mortgage at closing. These can be origination points (typically around one point) or discount points (negotiable). Each point costs one percent of the total purchase price of the house.

Like mortgage interest, mortgage points are tax deductible in the year you pay them. The cost of one point over 30 years is negligible, but if you move in two years and pay off the mortgage, one point would add 0.25% to the after-tax interest rate in the example above.

Home Equity Debt

A home equity loan is similarly tax deductible if it is taken out on your primary residence and used to buy or improve the home. It is deductible only to the extent the mortgage plus the home equity loan does not exceed $750,000.

Because it comes behind the first mortgage in repayment priority, home equity debt carries a slightly higher interest rate than a mortgage. Pre-tax interest rates are around 9%, which translate to 5-6% if you are a high-income taxpayer.

Home equity loans are for a fixed up-front amount and then are paid down over a period of two to five years. Because your payment goes mostly toward principal in the early years, the tax deduction is a small portion of the monthly payment initially and a large portion towards the end.

> *"HELOCs are a much less expensive alternative to revolving credit card debt"*

A home equity line of credit (HELOC) is more flexible because you can draw down or pay off the loan as you need it. If you have paid down your first mortgage by 20% or more, HELOCs are a much less expensive alternative to revolving credit card debt.

Margin Loans

There are two types of borrowing against stocks and bonds held at a brokerage – margin loans and non-purpose loans.

Margin loans are available directly from your broker in amounts up to 50% of the market value of your portfolio and can be used to purchase additional securities or for any other purpose.

If the value of your portfolio falls and the balance of the margin loan becomes more than 50% of the collateral, there is a margin call where you have to deposit more cash or sell some of your securities.

Margin loans are like revolving credit because you can draw or repay at any time. There are no minimum monthly payments or predetermined date by which you have to pay it back. Because they are collateralized by your investments, they are low risk and carry low interest rates – typically 10-12% at major brokerages.

The interest on margin loans is tax deductible against other *investment* income (but not against earned income), but only if you are able to itemize deductions before this interest expense. If you have other interest income, for example, your tax savings will reduce the effective interest cost on the loan by as much as 50%.

Margin loans can be used to purchase additional securities, but leverage increases the volatility of your investments and I don't recommend it. They can be used for short-term and variable cash needs of any type, but be careful not to fall into an ongoing cycle of debt.

The best uses of margin are (1) to pay off higher-rate non-deductible debt such as revolving credit card balances and (2) to delay having to sell appreciated securities and pay taxes on the capital gain, particularly *short-term* capital gain.

With a non-purpose loan, the lender is an external bank and the proceeds can be used for any purpose *except* buying securities. Non-purpose loans are often available in amounts greater than 50% of your portfolio, but they are more difficult to set up and typically not tax deductible. Margin loans are better.

Auto Loans

Car dealerships will negotiate the lowest price on a car or the lowest rate on a loan, but not both. So get the best price from the dealership and get the best loan at a bank or lender. Auto loans are generally amortizing fixed-rate loans with a down payment and terms between two and five years.

Despite the fact that the collateral – a new car – depreciates quickly once you drive it off the lot, auto loans have moderate interest rates of around 10-15%. Some auto manufacturers may offer lower interest rates as a promotion, so you may want to ask for the best financing rate from the dealer. The interest on auto loans is not tax deductible.

Personal Loans

Personal unsecured loans are offered by banks and online lenders like SoFi and Lending Club. Because they are not secured by assets like a house, car or securities, they carry higher interest rates and are not tax deductible.

Typically one- to five-year amortizing loans, they have interest rates that range from 15% to 30% depending primarily on your credit score.

These loans can be valuable for people looking for a more structured and lower-rate alternative to revolving credit card debt, and are sometimes used for debt consolidation.

Credit Cards

Credit card debt is often the most expensive alternative, with the exception of overdraft and subprime lending.

Credit card users are either transactors who pay off their balance every month or revolvers who don't. Transactors enjoy a free loan during the month prior to the payment date while revolvers pay interest on their balances from the day each purchase is made.

For revolvers, lower-cost credit cards charge around 20% while higher-cost cards charge as much as 30%. Late fees and other charges inflate the interest rates even higher.

Credit card interest is not tax deductible. If you consistently revolve on a credit card, it's time to find an alternative source of credit or tighten your budget.

Overdraft

Overdraft is absurdly expensive – even higher than predatory payday loans. Don't enable overdraft on your checking account and, if you do, be careful not to use it very often.

> *"Overdraft is absurdly expensive – even higher than predatory payday loans"*

Banks entice you to opt in for overdraft by saying it is a "courtesy" for when you overdraw your checking account by a small amount. But it's really a huge revenue generator for banks – overdraft fees totaled over $7 billion in bank revenues in 2022.

Typically, each time you overdraft you get charged $35 – up to three times a day – and you have to pay it back in a couple of days. A $25 overdraft, if repeated throughout the year, would result in an unthinkable compound interest rate.

- $25 overdraft debit card transaction
- $35 overdraft fee
- 140% interest over two days

- 12,740% interest over one year without compounding
  ($35 times 365/2 divided by $25)
- 39,382,428,521,284,700,000,000,000,000%
  compounded
  (140% to the power of 365/2)

To add insult to injury, overdraft interest and fees are not tax deductible.

Overdraft is usually used for small amounts and has a limited impact on each individual, but you may be amused by this story.

The Ballad of Duncan Hunter

Duncan was a congressman from San Diego. The FBI indicted him for stealing from his campaign funds. Why did he do it? Because he didn't have enough money of his own. (Of course.)

So, his personal checking account bounced along close to zero during the years the FBI was watching. When you have a low balance it's easy to fall below zero and get charged an overdraft fee.

During the period, he had 1,100 overdrafts. At $35 each, he paid almost $38,000 in overdraft fees.

Poor Duncan is an extreme example. But overdraft fees are a raw deal regardless of how often you use them.

State & Local Income Taxes

Where you live has a huge impact on how much of your income ends up going to taxes

State and local income taxes pile an additional tax bite on top of federal income taxes. In most cases, these taxes apply to investment income as well as earned income. Each of the states, as well as some counties, cities and towns, have their own tax rates and structure, but most follow the federal system for determining taxable income.

State Tax Structures

Thirty-two states and the District of Columbia have progressive tax structures, meaning the marginal tax rates increase on higher levels of income. The largest states with progressive structures are California and New York.

Twelve states have flat rates tax structures, where all taxable income is taxed at the same rate. The largest flat rate states are Pennsylvania and Illinois.

Seven states apply no state income tax at all, the largest being Texas and Florida. States with no income tax use sales and property taxes to fund government activities.

New Hampshire taxes only dividends and interest while Washington taxes only capital gains.

State Tax Rates

The states with the highest top marginal tax rates are:

13.30%	California
11.00%	Hawaii
10.75%	District of Columbia
10.75%	New Jersey
9.90%	Oregon
9.85%	Minnesota
9.65%	New York (higher for $5 million+)
9.00%	Massachusetts

Here are the top marginal state tax rates for single filers at various income levels in all 50 states and the District of Columbia, listed alphabetically. Additionally, the combined state and local tax rates for a few large high-tax cities are included:

| Alphabetical | Marginal Rate by Taxable Income | | | |
Single Taxpayer	$100k	$200k	$250k	$1,000k
Alabama	5.00%	5.00%	5.00%	5.00%
Alaska	0.00%	0.00%	0.00%	0.00%
Arizona	2.50%	2.50%	2.50%	2.50%
Arkansas	4.47%	4.47%	4.47%	4.47%
California	9.30%	9.30%	9.30%	13.30%
Colorado	4.40%	4.40%	4.40%	4.40%
Connecticut	6.00%	6.50%	6.90%	6.99%
Delaware	6.60%	6.60%	6.60%	6.60%
District of Columbia	8.50%	8.50%	9.25%	10.75%
Florida	0.00%	0.00%	0.00%	0.00%
Georgia	5.75%	5.75%	5.75%	5.75%
Hawaii	8.25%	11.00%	11.00%	11.00%
Idaho	5.80%	5.80%	5.80%	5.80%
Illinois	4.95%	4.95%	4.95%	4.95%
Indiana	3.15%	3.15%	3.15%	3.15%
Iowa	6.00%	6.00%	6.00%	6.00%
Kansas	5.70%	5.70%	5.70%	5.70%
Kentucky	4.50%	4.50%	4.50%	4.50%
Louisiana	4.25%	4.25%	4.25%	4.25%
Maine	7.15%	7.15%	7.15%	7.15%
Maryland	5.00%	5.50%	5.75%	5.75%
MD - Baltimore	8.20%	8.70%	8.95%	8.95%
Massachusetts	5.00%	5.00%	5.00%	9.00%
Michigan	4.05%	4.05%	4.05%	4.05%
Minnesota	7.85%	9.85%	9.85%	9.85%
Mississippi	5.00%	5.00%	5.00%	5.00%
Missouri	4.95%	4.95%	4.95%	4.95%
Montana	6.75%	6.75%	6.75%	6.75%
Nebraska	6.64%	6.64%	6.64%	6.64%

Nevada	0.00%	0.00%	0.00%	0.00%
New Hampshire *	4.00%	4.00%	4.00%	4.00%
New Jersey	6.37%	6.37%	6.37%	10.75%
New Mexico	4.90%	4.90%	5.90%	5.90%
New York **	6.00%	6.00%	6.85%	9.65%
NY - New York City	9.88%	9.88%	10.73%	13.53%
North Carolina	4.75%	4.75%	4.75%	4.75%
North Dakota	1.95%	1.95%	2.50%	2.50%
Ohio	3.69%	3.75%	3.75%	3.75%
Oklahoma	4.75%	4.75%	4.75%	4.75%
Oregon	8.75%	9.90%	9.90%	9.90%
OR - Portland	8.75%	12.40%	13.90%	13.90%
Pennsylvania	3.07%	3.07%	3.07%	3.07%
PA - Philadelphia	6.94%	6.94%	6.94%	6.94%
Rhode Island	4.75%	5.99%	5.99%	5.99%
South Carolina	6.50%	6.50%	6.50%	6.50%
South Dakota	0.00%	0.00%	0.00%	0.00%
Tennessee	0.00%	0.00%	0.00%	0.00%
Texas	0.00%	0.00%	0.00%	0.00%
Utah	4.65%	4.65%	4.65%	4.65%
Vermont	6.60%	7.60%	8.75%	8.75%
Virginia	5.75%	5.75%	5.75%	5.75%
Washington ***	7.00%	7.00%	7.00%	7.00%
West Virginia	5.12%	5.12%	5.12%	5.12%
Wisconsin	5.30%	5.30%	5.30%	7.65%
Wyoming	0.00%	0.00%	0.00%	0.00%

* NH interest & dividends only

** NY state top rate for >$1,007k (excl >5m income)

*** Washington capital gains only

Here are the tax rates organized from highest to lowest to show how they compare across different states and two key income levels: $250,000 and $1 million.

$250k Income Single Taxpayer	Tax Rate	$1,000k Income Single Taxpayer	Tax Rate
OR - Portland	13.90%	OR - Portland	13.90%
Hawaii	11.00%	NY - New York City	13.53%
NY - New York City	10.73%	California	13.30%
Oregon	9.90%	Hawaii	11.00%
Minnesota	9.85%	District of Columbia	10.75%
California	9.30%	New Jersey	10.75%
District of Columbia	9.25%	Oregon	9.90%
MD - Baltimore	8.95%	Minnesota	9.85%
Vermont	8.75%	New York	9.65%
Maine	7.15%	Massachusetts	9.00%
Washington **	7.00%	MD - Baltimore	8.95%
PA - Philadelphia	6.94%	Vermont	8.75%
Connecticut	6.90%	Wisconsin	7.65%
New York	6.85%	Maine	7.15%
Montana	6.75%	Washington **	7.00%
Nebraska	6.64%	Connecticut	6.99%
Delaware	6.60%	PA - Philadelphia	6.94%
South Carolina	6.50%	Montana	6.75%
New Jersey	6.37%	Nebraska	6.64%
Iowa	6.00%	Delaware	6.60%
Rhode Island	5.99%	South Carolina	6.50%
New Mexico	5.90%	Iowa	6.00%
Idaho	5.80%	Rhode Island	5.99%
Georgia	5.75%	New Mexico	5.90%
Maryland	5.75%	Idaho	5.80%
Virginia	5.75%	Georgia	5.75%
Kansas	5.70%	Maryland	5.75%
Wisconsin	5.30%	Virginia	5.75%
West Virginia	5.12%	Kansas	5.70%

Including federal taxes, a single filer with $200,000 taxable income residing in California would pay 9.3% state, plus 35% federal, plus 3.8% NIIT, for a total tax rate of 48.1% on each additional dollar of interest income.

Local Income Taxes

A significant number of counties, cities and other jurisdictions charge their own income tax in addition to federal and state rates. The largest high-tax cities are:

	State Tax	Local Tax	Total Tax
Portland, OR	9.9%	4.0%	13.9%
New York City, NY *	9.6%	3.9%	13.5%
Baltimore, MD	5.7%	3.2%	8.9%
Philadelphia, PA	3.1%	3.8%	6.9%

* Higher for incomes over $5 million

Residents of Portland pay combined tax for Oregon state, Portland metro and Multnomah county. The top marginal rate of 13.9% applies to single taxpayers with incomes over $250,000 and married filing jointly with incomes over $400,000. Portland has the highest state and local income tax in the country.

Estate and Inheritance Taxes

Estate taxes, paid by the estate's owner, depend on the total estate value. Inheritance taxes, paid by the heir, are based on what each beneficiary receives.

2023 State Estate and Inheritance Tax

	Estate Tax Rates	Estate Tax Exemption
Connecticut	12.0%	$12,920,000
DC	11.2 - 16.0%	$4,528,800
Hawaii	10.0 - 20.0%	$5,490,000
Illinois	0.8 - 16.0%	$4,000,000
Maine	8.0 - 12.0%	$6,410,000
Maryland *	0.8 - 16.0%	$5,000,000
Massachusetts	0.8 - 16.0%	$2,000,000
Minnesota	13.0 - 16.0%	$3,000,000
New York	3.06 - 16.0%	$6,580,000
Oregon	10.0 - 16.0%	$1,000,000
Rhode Island	0.8 - 16.0%	$1,733,264
Vermont	16.0%	$5,000,000
Washington	10.0 - 20.0%	$2,193,000

	Inheritance Tax Rates	Inheritance Exemption
Iowa	0.0 - 6.0%	Varied
Kentucky	0.0 - 16.0%	Varied
Maryland *	0.0 - 10.0%	Varied
Nebraska	0.0 - 15.0%	Varied
New Jersey	0.0 - 16.0%	Varied
Pennsylvania	0.0 - 15.0%	Varied

* Maryland has both an estate tax and an inheritance tax.

Property Taxes

In the US, state and local municipalities set the property tax rates, which can vary significantly based on where you live. The *effective property tax rate* is a useful concept to give you a clearer picture of the average property tax rate you face. It's calculated by dividing the total property taxes paid in a state by the total home value of owner-occupied homes.

> *"New Jersey has the highest effective real estate tax rate at 2.23%."*

Highest Effective Property Tax Rate and Median Annual Bill

State	Tax Rate	Tax Bill
New Jersey	2.23%	$9,499
Illinois	2.08%	$5,721
New Hampshire	1.93%	$7,698
Vermont	1.83%	$6,207
Connecticut	1.79%	$6,082

Lowest Effective Property Tax Rate and Median Annual Bill

State	Tax Rate	Tax Bill
Hawaii	0.32%	$2,306
Alabama	0.40%	$1,038
Colorado	0.55%	$3,081
Louisiana	0.56%	$1,369
Wyoming	0.56%	$1,525

Sales Taxes

Depending on where you live in the US, the sales tax you pay might look quite different. In 45 states, there's a state-level sales tax and, in 38 of those, local taxes come into play too. So, even if your state has a moderate state tax, the total rate could jump up once local taxes are added.

Highest State Sales Tax		Lowest State Sales Tax	
State	Sales Tax Rate	State	Sales Tax Rate
California	7.25%	Oregon	0.00%
Tennessee	7.00%	New Hampshire	0.00%
Rhode Island	7.00%	Montana	0.00%
Mississippi	7.00%	Delaware	0.00%
Indiana	7.00%	Alaska	0.00%

Tax Burden

A metric known as *tax burden* measures the average percentage of total personal income taken by taxes of all types of state and local taxes, including income tax, property tax and sales tax.

As calculated by WalletHub, the states with the highest total tax burdens are similar – but not identical – to those among the highest income tax rates: New York, Hawaii, Maine, Vermont and Connecticut. Despite having the highest top marginal income tax rate, California is only 12th highest in overall tax burden.

Of the largest states with no state income tax, Florida ranks 46th in tax burden. However, Texas ranks 29th due to high property and sales taxes.

Highest Total State Tax Burden		**Lowest** Total State Tax Burden	
State	Total Tax Burden	State	Total Tax Burden
New York	12.47%	Alaska	5.06%
Hawaii	12.31%	Delaware	6.12%
Maine	11.14%	New Hampshire	6.14%
Vermont	10.28%	Tennessee	6.22%
Connecticut	9.83%	Florida	6.33%

Non-Resident State Income Tax

Each state has its own set of rules regarding tax on earned income – salary, freelance and unincorporated business income – for non-residents, which generally fall into four categories.

States with Reciprocity Agreements

In these states, there are agreements that allow residents to pay income tax only to their home state, not the state where they work. This simplifies tax filing and reduces the tax burden for cross-border workers. Here's how they work:

- **Taxation only in the resident state:** If you live in one state and work in another, you only have to pay income tax to your resident state. The state where you work typically does not tax your income.

- **No need for tax credits for out-of-state taxes:** Because you're only paying income tax to your resident state, there's no need for a tax credit for taxes paid to the state where you work. This is different from non-reciprocal states, where you might pay tax to both states but receive a credit from your resident state to offset the tax paid to the work state.

There are currently 30 reciprocal agreements across 16 states and the District of Columbia.

State	Reciprocal Agreement
Arizona	California, Indiana, Oregon, Virginia
District of Columbia	All nonresidents who work DC can claim exemption from DC income tax
Illinois	Iowa, Kentucky, Michigan, Wisconsin
Indiana	Kentucky, Michigan, Ohio, Pennsylvania, Wisconsin
Iowa	Illinois
Kentucky	Illinois, Indiana, Michigan, Ohio, West Virginia, Wisconsin, Virginia
Maryland	District of Columbia, Pennsylvania, Virginia, West Virginia
Michigan	Wisconsin, Indiana, Kentucky, Illinois, Ohio, Minnesota
Minnesota	Michigan, North Dakota
Montana	North Dakota
New Jersey	Pennsylvania
North Dakota	Minnesota, Montana
Ohio	Indiana, Kentucky, Michigan, Pennsylvania, West Virginia
Pennsylvania	Indiana, Maryland, New Jersey, Ohio, Virginia, West Virginia
Virginia	Kentucky, Maryland, District of Columbia, Pennsylvania, West Virginia

| West Virginia | Kentucky, Maryland, Ohio, Pennsylvania, Virginia |
| Wisconsin | Illinois, Indiana, Kentucky, Michigan |

States Without Reciprocity Agreements

In the 25 states without reciprocal agreements, individuals typically must file tax returns in both their home state and the state where they work. They may receive a credit in their home state for taxes paid to the work state to avoid double taxation. Here's how it works:

- **Tax liability in both states:** If you live in one state and work in another, you are generally subject to state income tax in both states.

- **Pay taxes to the work state:** You will pay taxes to the state where you work on the earned income you received from working there.

- **File and pay taxes in your home state:** You will also file a tax return in your home state, where you are taxed on your worldwide income, including the income earned in the work state.

- **Tax credit to prevent double taxation:** Your home state typically offers a tax credit for the taxes you paid to the work state. However, this credit is usually limited to the amount of tax you would have paid on that income at your home state's tax rate.

- **Paying the higher tax rate:** Regardless of whether you live in the higher-tax state and work in the lower-tax state, or vice versa, you will ultimately pay the higher of the two states' tax rates on your income.

"Without reciprocity, you'll ultimately pay the higher of the two states' tax rates."

States with Reverse Tax Credits

In this less common system, the work state offers a credit for taxes paid to the resident state. For example, if an Arizona resident works in California, they pay Arizona state taxes, and California then credits them for these taxes. However, the taxpayer may still owe taxes to California if its tax rate is higher than Arizona's. This does not eliminate the need to file in both states, and the taxpayer is still subject to the higher tax rate of the two states.

States Without Any Income Tax

If an individual lives in a state that does not levy state income tax but works in a state that does tax income, they will only need to pay state income tax in the state where they work. Conversely, if they live in a state with income tax but work in a state without, they only pay income tax to their home state.

Alabama

The Yellowhammer State has the nation's second-lowest effective property tax rate.

Alabama, whose nickname hails from the Civil War era when its troops donned uniforms adorned with bright yellow cloth, is not just rich in historical color. The state also offers competitive income tax rates, ranging from 2% to 5%. These rates apply to ordinary income as well as capital gains.

Taxpayers can claim both a standard deduction and a personal exemption to lower taxable income. The standard deduction depends on income: Single taxpayers can claim between $2,500 and $3,000 and married couples filing jointly can claim between $5,000 and $8,500.

Each individual can claim a $1,500 personal exemption, and based on the taxpayer's adjusted gross income, can claim $300 to $1,000 for each dependent. A head of household with a qualifying dependent is allowed a $3,000 exemption.

Alabama also has an extensive list of tax-exempt income streams, such as certain pension benefits, Social Security benefits, unemployment compensation, child support, military pay, and insurance proceeds.

The other good news is that Alabama does not levy an estate or inheritance tax.

Alabama Income Tax Rates

Rates apply to income between that bracket and the next highest bracket

2023 Tax Rates	Single Taxpayer	Married Filing Jointly	Married Filing Separately	Head of Household
2.00%	$0	$0	$0	$0
4.00%	$500	$1,000	$500	$500
5.00%	$3,000	$6,000	$3,000	$3,000

Property Tax

In Alabama, with an effective property tax rate of 0.40% and a median home value of $259,538.73, homeowners face an annual tax bill of approximately $1,038.14.

State and Local Sales Tax

Alabama has a 4% state sales tax, with local governments having the liberty to impose an extra tax up to 7.5%. However, certain items, including prescription drugs, gasoline, motor oil, seeds for planting, and livestock, are typically exempt from this sales tax.

Non-Resident State Income Tax

In Alabama, residents and non-residents working across state lines pay the higher of the two states' income tax rates, due to the absence of reciprocal agreements.

Alaska

The Last Frontier State has no state income tax and claims the nation's lowest tax burden.

Alaska, aptly nicknamed for its unspoiled and expansive wilderness, further echoes this spirit of freedom and self-reliance by being one of the few states in America where residents do not pay taxes on personal income, capital gains, estates, or inheritances.

However, residents might still have to deal with other types of taxes, like property tax and sales tax. The rates for these taxes could change based on where you live and where you buy products or use services.

"Alaska does not have a state income tax."

Property Tax

In Alaska, with an effective property tax rate of 1.04% and a median home value of $349,474.30, homeowners face an annual tax bill of approximately $3,636.72.

State and Local Sales Tax

Even though Alaska doesn't levy any sales taxes, certain municipalities impose local taxes. These local sales tax rates can reach up to 7.5%, but the average is just 1.813%.

Non-Resident State Income Tax

Alaska has no state income tax. Alaska residents working in other states pay income taxes to those states. Non-residents working in Alaska pay income taxes to their own states.

STATE INCOME TAX

Arizona

The Grand Canyon State has the 10th-lowest effective property tax rate in the country.

Arizona can be a beautiful place to reside year-round, especially with the Grand Canyon and other national monuments conveniently located throughout the state.

Another perk of living in Arizona is its competitive individual income tax rate. Starting in 2023, Arizona implemented a flat income tax of 2.5%, which applies to ordinary income as well as capital gains.

To ease the tax burden, Arizona offers its taxpayers a standard deduction equal to $13,850 for individuals and $27,700 for married couples filing jointly.

Additionally, there are no estate or inheritance taxes in Arizona.

"Arizona levies a flat income tax rate of 2.5%, regardless of filing status or income."

Property Tax

In Arizona, with an effective property tax rate of 0.63% and a median home value of $425,544.41, homeowners face an annual tax bill of approximately $2,662.11.

State and Local Sales Tax

Arizona imposes a state sales tax rate of 5.6% and permits local governments to levy a local option sales tax of up to 5.3%. The specific rate applied to your goods and services depends on the county purchased in. Certain items are excluded from sales tax, like groceries and prescription goods.

Non-Resident State Income Tax

Arizona residents working in states like California, Indiana, Oregon, and Virginia, and residents of these states working in Arizona, pay income tax solely to their home state, thanks to reciprocal agreements.

STATE INCOME TAX

Arkansas

The Natural State has two tax bracket sets: one for incomes over $84,500 and one for those below.

Arkansas, known for its stunning lakes, rivers, wildlife, and mountains, has earned its nickname from this picturesque scenery.

The state uses a dual tax rate system based on individual net income: one set of rates for those earning $84,500 or less, and another set for those earning more than $84,500. To help ease the tax burden, individual taxpayers can claim a standard deduction of $2,270, while married couples filing jointly are entitled to a $4,540 deduction.

Arkansas Income Tax Rates

Rates apply to income between each bracket and the next higher bracket

2023 Tax Rates	Tax Bracket
Income < $84,500	
0.00%	$0
2.00%	$5,099
3.00%	$10,299
3.40%	$14,699
4.70%	$24,299
Income > $84,500	
2.00%	$0
4.00%	$4,400
4.47%	$8,800

Arkansas has no estate or inheritance taxes.

Capital Gains Tax

Arkansas offers specific advantages for capital gains: up to 50% of net capital gains are exempt from state taxation, and any capital gains over $10 million are free from ordinary income taxes.

Property Tax

In Arkansas, with an effective property tax rate of 0.64% and a median home value of $319,951.59, homeowners face an annual tax bill of approximately $2,054.45.

State and Local Sales Tax

Arkansas imposes a sales tax rate of 6.5% on tangible personal property. Counties can also enforce their own tax, up to 6.125%. This can make your total tax rate nearly 13% on some purchases. There are exemptions to Arkansas' state sales tax rate, such as sewer services, electricity, and energy.

Non-Resident State Income Tax

Arkansas does not have reciprocal agreements, leading to residents and non-residents working in the state paying the higher tax rate of either Arkansas or their home state.

STATE INCOME TAX

California

The Golden State tops the charts with the nation's highest state income tax rates.

In 2023, California earned its Golden State title with the highest state income tax rates in the country, potentially totaling 54.1% with federal taxes on specific income.

California's maximum rates are 12.3% plus a 1% mental health tax on high-income taxpayers for a total 13.3% marginal tax rate – the tax you pay on your next dollar of income. The specific marginal tax rates, which vary according to income brackets, are uniformly applied to almost all types of income, including salary, bonus, interest, dividends, long-term capital gains, and short-term capital gains.

The only types of income not subject to California state tax are Treasury bonds, some municipal bonds, and distributions from certain tax-deferred accounts. Despite California's high tax rates, the state offers tax relief through standard deductions and personal exemption credits to ease the tax burden. Single taxpayers or those married filing separately can claim a standard deduction of $5,202, while those married filing jointly or as head of household can claim $10,404.

Personal exemption credits are also available: $140 for individuals, $280 for married couples filing jointly, and $433 for dependents.

California residents can also take comfort in the fact that there are no estate or inheritance taxes.

California Income Tax Rates

Rates apply to income between that bracket and the next highest bracket

2023 Tax Rates	Single Taxpayer	Married Filing Jointly	Married Filing Separately	Head of Household
1.00%	$0	$0	$0	$0
2.00%	$10,412	$20,824	$10,412	$20,839
4.00%	$24,684	$49,368	$24,684	$49,371
6.00%	$38,959	$77,918	$38,959	$63,644
8.00%	$54,081	$108,162	$54,081	$78,765
9.30%	$68,350	$136,700	$68,350	$93,037
10.30%	$349,137	$698,274	$349,137	$474,824
11.30%	$418,961	$837,922	$418,961	$569,790
12.30%	$698,271	$1,000,000	$698,271	$949,549
13.30%	$1,000,000	$1,396,542	$1,000,000	$1,000,000

Property Tax

In California, with an effective property tax rate of 0.75% and a median home value of $750,079.85, homeowners face an annual tax bill of approximately $5,602.79.

Sales and Local Sales Tax

California's statewide sales tax rate is 7.25%. Local sales tax rates that vary by district and can add up to another 4.75%.

Non-Resident State Income Tax

California, lacking reciprocal agreements, requires residents working in other states and non-residents working in California to pay the higher of the two states' income tax rates.

STATE INCOME TAX

Colorado

The Centennial State has the third-lowest effective property tax rate in the nation.

Colorado earned its nickname, the Centennial State, as it became a state exactly 100 years after the signing of the Declaration of Independence. Known for its spectacular views, Colorado also boasts a straightforward flat income tax rate of 4.4%, which applies to ordinary income as well as capital gains.

> *"Colorado levies a flat income tax rate of 4.4%, regardless of filing status or income."*

Colorado also allows standard deductions to provide taxpayers with some tax relief. Married couples filing jointly can claim $27,700; single taxpayers and married individuals filing separately can claim $13,850; and heads of households can claim $20,800. These deductions are limited once income exceeds $300,000.

Additionally, there are no estate or inheritance taxes to worry about in Colorado.

Property Tax

In Colorado, with an effective property tax rate of 0.55% and a median home value of $563,896.47, homeowners face an annual tax bill of approximately $3,080.83.

State and Local Sales Tax

Colorado imposes a 2.9% sales tax rate on sales made within the state. In addition, retailers must also collect an additional $0.27 delivery fee on every sale that is delivered by motor vehicle. Colorado also has many cities and countries that have local taxes in place. These rates are capped at 8.3%. The highest combined state and local sales tax burden is found in the city of Winter Park at 11.2%. The lowest combined rates are found in Cheyenne County and Kiowa County at 7.8%.

Non-Resident State Income Tax

Colorado's absence of reciprocal agreements means residents working in other states and non-residents working in Colorado ultimately pay the higher of the two states' tax rates.

STATE INCOME TAX

Connecticut

The Constitution State's heavy overall tax burden can present challenges for high earners.

Connecticut earned its nickname by creating one of the earliest written constitutions for democratic government in 1639.

Connecticut has three different tax tables based on your filing status, with taxes up to 6.99%. Furthermore, the state taxes capital gains at the same rate as ordinary income.

Connecticut provides tax exemptions for most taxpayers that eliminate taxes on the first dollars of income – up to $15,000 for single filers, $12,000 for married individuals filing separately, $19,000 for heads of household, and $24,000 for married couples filing jointly. These exemptions begin to phase out when adjusted gross income exceeds $30,000 for single filers, $24,000 for married couples filing separately, $38,000 for heads of households, and $48,000 for married couples filing jointly.

Conecticut Income Tax Rates
Rates apply to income between that bracket and the next highest bracket

2023 Tax Rates	Single Taxpayer	Married Filing Jointly	Married Filing Separately	Head of Household
3.00%	$0	$0	$0	$0
5.00%	$10,000	$20,000	$10,000	$16,000
5.50%	$50,000	$100,000	$50,000	$80,000
6.00%	$100,000	$200,000	$100,000	$160,000
6.50%	$200,000	$400,000	$200,000	$320,000
6.90%	$250,000	$500,000	$250,000	$400,000
6.99%	$500,000	$1,000,000	$500,000	$800,000

Estate and Inheritance Taxes
Connecticut levies a 12% estate tax, however, estates valued up to $12,920,000 are exempt. Essentially, if your estate's worth does not exceed this figure, you're not liable for estate tax. And no inheritance tax exists in Connecticut, offering heirs notable tax advantages.

Property Tax
In Connecticut, with an effective property tax rate of 1.79% and a median home value of $339,838.28, homeowners face an annual tax bill of approximately $6,082.22.

State and Local Sales Tax
Connecticut levies a 6.35% state sales tax rate on most goods sold within the state. Vehicles over $50,000 are subject to a rate of 7.75%. Since the general sales and use tax rate is so high, Connecticut doesn't allow additional local taxes other than property taxes to be assessed by counties.

Non-Resident State Income Tax

Connecticut does not have reciprocal agreements, leading to residents and non-residents working in the state being subject to the higher tax rate of either Connecticut or their home state.

STATE INCOME TAX

Delaware

Moderate income tax, no sales tax, and low property taxes make the First State tax-friendly.

Delaware was the first state to ratify the U.S. Constitution, creating the state's nickname. Along with its rich history, Delaware is one of the few states to impose a single set of brackets for all filing statuses.

If you earn less than $2,000, you won't have to pay any taxes. But if your income goes above $60,000, you'll be in the top tax bracket with a rate of 6.60%. The same rate applies to capital gains as it does to ordinary income.

Delaware offers residents a standard deduction to lower their taxable income. The standard deduction is $6,500 for married couples filing jointly and $3,250 all other filers. Delaware imposes few additional taxes, boasting one of the lowest average property tax rates in the country.

Furthermore, the state doesn't charge sales or use taxes on individuals and doesn't have estate or inheritance taxes.

Delaware Income Tax Rates

Rates apply to income between each bracket and the next higher bracket

2023 Tax Rates	Tax Bracket
0.00%	$0
2.20%	$2,000
3.90%	$5,000
4.80%	$10,000
5.20%	$20,000
5.55%	$25,000
6.60%	$60,000

Property Tax

In Delaware, with an effective property tax rate of 0.61% and a median home value of $349,990.75, homeowners face an annual tax bill of approximately $2,146.41.

State and Local Sales Tax

Delaware is one of the unique states that doesn't impose any state or local sales tax. However, these taxes are made up for through assessments of businesses.

Non-Resident State Income Tax

Delaware residents working in other states and non-residents working in Delaware ultimately pay the higher of the two states' income tax rates, due to the lack of reciprocal agreements.

STATE INCOME TAX

District of Columbia

DC has high income tax rates and relatively low property taxes.

The District of Columbia is not considered a state or part of any state. Instead, DC is a federal district in the control of the U.S. Congress in Washington, DC.

DC uses a graduated-rate tax system with rates ranging from 4% to 10.75%, which apply to ordinary income as well as capital gains.

However, residents can take the federal standard deduction to reduce taxable income: $13,850 for single filers and married individuals filing separately, $27,700 for married couples filing jointly, and $20,800 for heads of households.

District of Columbia Income Tax

Rates apply to income between each bracket and the next higher bracket

2023 Tax Rates	Tax Bracket
4.00%	$0
6.00%	$10,000
6.50%	$40,000
8.50%	$60,000
9.25%	$250,000
9.75%	$500,000
10.75%	$1,000,000

Estate and Inheritance Taxes

In DC, estates valued at $4,528,800 or less are exempt from estate tax. For those exceeding this amount, the tax rates vary between 11.2% and 16%. However, DC doesn't have an inheritance tax, which means heirs can benefit from significant tax savings.

Property Tax

In the District of Columbia, with an effective property tax rate of 0.62% and a median home value of $649,721.52, homeowners face an annual tax bill of approximately $4,035.59.

State and Local Sales Tax

DC only has one sales tax rate, which is 6%. Since DC is not considered a state, there are no territories or jurisdictions that can impose additional local taxes. However, tickets to theaters and entertainment venues are taxed at 8%.

Non-Resident State Income Tax

All non-residents working in the District of Columbia can claim exemption from DC income tax, paying taxes only to their home state. But this only works in reverse with two states: Maryland and Virginia. You don't have to file a nonresident return in either of these states if you live in DC but work in either of these states.

STATE INCOME TAX

Florida

The Sunshine State has no income tax and claims the fifth-lowest overall tax burden in the nation.

Florida offers more than an ideal destination for vacations, part-time living, and relaxation. In fact, Florida is one the few states that doesn't impose taxes on personal income, capital gains, estates, or inheritances.

> *"Florida does not have a state income tax."*

However, Florida does earn tax revenue from other sources, such as state and local sales tax and property taxes. Taxpayers residing in Florida do not need to file an individual income tax return, but are typically required to file federal income tax returns, depending on income levels.

Property Tax

In Florida, with an effective property tax rate of 0.91% and a median home value of $361,918.02, homeowners face an annual tax bill of approximately $3,302.82.

State and Local Sales Tax

The state sales tax rate in Florida is 6%. There are a few exceptions to this rule, including a rate of 3% for retail sales of new mobile homes, 4% for amusement machines, and 5.5% for the rent or lease of commercial real property. Electricity is also subject to a higher state sales tax rate of 6.95%. Taxpayers may also find themselves subject to local sales tax, which is capped at 2% per county. You can expect most counties to implement a rate around 1%, making your total state and local sales tax burden of around 7%.

Non-Resident State Income Tax

Florida has no state income tax. Florida residents working in other states pay income taxes to those states. Non-residents working in Florida pay income taxes to their own states.

STATE INCOME TAX

Georgia

Most full-time workers in the Empire State of the South face the highest state income tax rate.

Georgia, historically known as the Empire State of the South for its pre-Civil War industrial growth and large land area, currently has a progressive tax system with rates from 1% to 5.75%. In 2024, it will shift to a flat tax rate of 5.49%, aiming to lower it to 4.99% by 2029.

Georgia has standard deductions and personal exemptions that taxpayers can claim to reduce their taxable income. The standard deduction is $5,400 for individual and head of household filers and $7,100 for married couples filing jointly. The personal exemption is $2,700 for individual taxpayers, $7,400 for married couples filing jointly, and $3,000 for each eligible dependent.

And while there are no estate or inheritance taxes, capital gains are not exempt from taxation – they're subject to the same rates as ordinary income.

Georgia Income Tax Rates

Rates apply to income between each bracket and the next higher bracket

2023 Tax Rates	Tax Bracket
1.00%	$0
2.00%	$750
3.00%	$2,250
4.00%	$3,750
5.00%	$5,250
5.75%	$7,000

Property Tax

In Georgia, with an effective property tax rate of 0.92% and a median home value of $350,471.23, homeowners face an annual tax bill of approximately $3,228.09.

State and Local Sales Tax

Georgia has a state sales tax rate of 4% and a maximum local sales tax rate of 5%. This means your total tax assessed on purchases can reach 9%. The local sales tax rates are released on a quarterly basis and can change depending on the county's needs.

Non-Resident State Income Tax

Georgia, without reciprocal agreements, requires both residents working in other states and non-residents working in Georgia to pay the higher of the two states' income tax rates.

STATE INCOME TAX

Hawaii

The Aloha State has the nation's lowest effective property tax, but high earners face top tax rates.

Hawaii is known for its warm and welcoming residents who greet tourists with "aloha," meaning "hello" in Hawaiian.

However, Hawaii has some of the highest state income tax rates in the nation, with the top rate reaching 11%. Combined with the federal top tax bracket and you can find yourself paying almost 50% of your income in taxes.

The good news is that Hawaii does have personal exemptions and standard deductions that you can use to reduce your taxable income. For 2023, the standard deduction is $2,200 for individuals, $3,212 for heads of households, and $4,400 for married couples filing jointly. The personal exemption is $1,144 for individuals, $2,288 for married couples filing jointly, and $1,144 per dependent.

Hawaii Income Tax Rates

Rates apply to income between that bracket and the next highest bracket

2023 Tax Rates	Single Taxpayer	Married Filing Jointly	Married Filing Separately	Head of Household
1.40%	$0	$0	$0	$0
3.20%	$2,400	$4,800	$2,400	$3,600
5.50%	$4,800	$9,600	$4,800	$7,200
6.40%	$9,600	$19,200	$9,600	$14,400
6.80%	$14,400	$28,800	$14,400	$21,600
7.20%	$19,200	$38,400	$19,200	$28,800
7.60%	$24,000	$48,000	$24,000	$36,000
7.90%	$36,000	$72,000	$36,000	$54,000
8.25%	$48,000	$96,000	$48,000	$72,000
9.00%	$150,000	$300,000	$150,000	$225,000
10.00%	$175,000	$350,000	$175,000	$262,000
11.00%	$200,000	$400,000	$200,000	$300,000

Capital Gains Tax

Unlike many states that tax capital gains at the same rate as ordinary income, Hawaii sets a distinct rate of 7.25% for long-term capital gains. This approach offers an advantage if you are a higher income individual, as you pay a reduced rate on your capital gains compared to your ordinary income.

Estate and Inheritance Taxes

Hawaii imposes an estate tax with rates between 10% to 20%. Yet, estates valued at $5,490,000 or less are exempt. This means if your estate's value is below this threshold, you won't owe any estate tax. On the other hand, Hawaii doesn't have an inheritance tax, which can provide significant tax benefits for heirs.

Property Tax

In Hawaii, with an effective property tax rate of 0.32% and a median home value of $731,779.92, homeowners face an average annual tax bill of approximately $2,306.30.

State and Local Sales Tax

Hawaii has a 4% state sales tax rate and a maximum 0.50% local sales tax rate. This brings your maximum state and local sales tax total to 4.5%. Oahu County, Kauai County, and Hawaii County currently leverage the additional 0.50% local state tax rate.

Non-Resident State Income Tax

Hawaii does not have reciprocal agreements, so residents working elsewhere and non-residents working in Hawaii pay the higher of the two states' income tax rates.

STATE INCOME TAX

Idaho

The Gem State has a flat income tax and a relatively low effective property tax rate.

Idaho, known as the Gem State for its mineral-rich terrain, introduced a flat 5.8% income tax, starting January 3, 2023. This rate applies to both ordinary income and capital gains.

> *"Idaho levies a flat income tax rate of 5.8%."*

Idaho offers a standard deduction aligned with federal standards, ranging from $13,850 for single filers and those married filing separately to $27,700 for couples filing jointly and $20,800 for heads of households.

Additionally, the state doesn't impose estate or inheritance taxes.

Property Tax

In Idaho, with an effective property tax rate of 0.67% and a median home value of $494,886.28, homeowners face an annual tax bill of approximately $3,292.08.

State and Local Sales Tax

Idaho levies a 6% state sales tax rate on most purchases. Counties also can impose local sales tax rates up to 3%. Some counties have local sales tax rates as low as 0.1%, while others, like Blaine County, max out the 3%.

Non-Resident State Income Tax

In Idaho, without reciprocal tax agreements, both residents working in other states and non-residents working in Idaho pay the higher tax rate of the two states involved.

STATE INCOME TAX

Illinois

The Land of Lincoln has a heavy tax burden, fueled by its property, income, and sales taxes rates.

Illinois, known as the Land of Lincoln where Abraham Lincoln began his political journey, also adopts a straightforward fiscal approach, applying a flat tax rate of 4.95% to ordinary income as well as capital gains.

Illinois provides numerous ways for residents to reduce their taxable income, one of which is through personal exemptions. For 2023, individuals can claim a $2,425 personal exemption, which completely phases out with an adjusted gross income of $250,000. Married couples filing jointly can claim a $4,850 personal exemption, which phases out at $500,000. Taxpayers that are over the age of 65 or legally blind can claim an additional $1,000 exemption. With personal exemptions, your tax bill could be eliminated if your income is below the threshold.

> *"Illinois levies a flat income tax rate of 4.95%, regardless of filing status or income."*

Estate and Inheritance Taxes
In Illinois, the estate tax rates range from 0.8% to 16%. However, if an estate's value is $4,000,000 or less, it's exempt from this tax. However, the state does not levy an inheritance tax.

Property Tax
In Illinois, with an effective property tax rate of 2.08% and a median home value of $274,731.33, homeowners face an annual tax bill of approximately $5,720.81.

State and Local Sales Tax

Most Illinois purchases are subject to a 6.25% state sales tax rate. However, certain foods, drugs, and medical appliances receive a reduced rate of 1%. Individual municipalities can also levy a local tax on purchases, up to 4.75%. This brings the potential total tax assessed to 11%. Counties, like Robinson and Momence, don't have local sales tax provisions in place, while others, like Harvey and Harwood Heights, have local rates of over 4%.

Non-Resident State Income Tax

Illinois residents working in Iowa, Kentucky, Michigan, and Wisconsin, and vice versa, are only taxed by their home state, thanks to reciprocal agreements.

STATE INCOME TAX

Indiana

The Hoosier State's income tax rate is reasonable, but local taxes can add to the tax burden.

In Indiana, the nickname Hoosier State reflects its friendly culture, stemming from the historical tradition of residents calling out "Who's yere?" to visitors at the door.

This simplicity extends to the state's tax system, which follows a low flat tax rate of 3.15%, which applies to ordinary income as well as capital gains.

Indiana has personal exemptions that can reduce your taxable income. Individuals can claim a $1,000 exemption and married couples filing jointly can claim a $2,000 exemption in 2023. If you report dependents, you can also claim an additional $1,000 per dependent.

> *"Indiana levies a flat income tax rate of 3.15%, regardless of filing status or income level."*

In addition, Indiana doesn't have estate or inheritance taxes.

Property Tax
In Indiana, with an effective property tax rate of 0.84% and a median home value of $250,000.12, homeowners face an annual tax bill of approximately $2,107.97.

State and Local Sales Tax
Indiana assesses a 7% state sales tax on most purchases. However, they do not allow any local sales tax to be charged in counties. Certain items, like groceries and prescription drugs, are exempt from the 7% sales tax rate.

Non-Resident State Income Tax
Indiana's reciprocal agreements with Kentucky, Michigan, Ohio, Pennsylvania, and Wisconsin allow residents of these states working in Indiana, and Indiana residents working in

these states, to pay state taxes only to their respective home states.

STATE INCOME TAX

Iowa

The Hawkeye State's income and property taxes are above average, while sales taxes are moderate.

Known as the Hawkeye State in honor of Chief Black Hawk, a Sauk tribe leader, Iowa also demonstrates a commitment to its residents through tax reforms. The state reduced the top income tax rate from 8.53% to 6% in 2023, applicable to both ordinary income and capital gains.

However, due to the recent tax rate decrease, Iowa no longer offers its residents a standard deduction.

Iowa Income Tax Rates
Rates apply to income between that bracket and the next highest bracket

2023 Tax Rates	Single Taxpayer	Married Filing Jointly	Married Filing Separately	Head of Household
4.40%	$0	$0	$0	$0
4.82%	$6,000	$12,000	$6,000	$6,000
5.70%	$30,000	$60,000	$30,000	$30,000
6.00%	$75,000	$150,000	$75,000	$75,000

Estate and Inheritance Taxes

Iowa does not have an estate tax, but the state does have an inheritance tax, which could be anywhere between 2% and 6%. It actually depends on how much you're getting and how closely related you are to the person who passed away. If you're the surviving spouse, stepchild, or directly related (like a child, grandchild, parent, or grandparent), you don't have to pay any inheritance tax. And if the entire estate is worth less than $25,000, there's no tax either.

Property Tax

In Iowa, with an effective property tax rate of 1.52% and a median home value of $248,259.88, homeowners face an annual tax bill of approximately $3,783.72.

State and Local Sales Tax

Iowa also has both sales and use taxes. Sales tax is currently assessed at a rate of 6%, with an additional 1% local sales tax applying to most purchases. The average combined state and local sales tax rate is 6.94%. The maximum rate is 7%.

Non-Resident State Income Tax

Iowa's reciprocal agreement with Illinois permits residents of Iowa working in Illinois, and Illinois residents working in Iowa, to pay state taxes only to their respective home states.

Kansas

The Sunflower State has the ninth-highest combined state and local sales tax in the nation.

Centuries ago, American Indians in Kansas relied on the native sunflower for sustenance. Embracing this legacy, Kansas declared the sunflower its official emblem in 1903 and proudly named itself the Sunflower State.

Today's Kansans pay taxes on a progressive scale, with rates from 0% to 5.70%, which apply to both ordinary income and capital gains.

When it comes to deductions, individual taxpayers can subtract $3,500 from their income, heads of households get a $6,000 deduction, and married couples filing jointly can deduct $8,000. Plus, all residents can take a $2,250 personal exemption, which doubles to $4,500 for heads of households, joint-filing couples, and honorably discharged military members.

Additionally, the state does not levy any estate or inheritance taxes.

Kansas Income Tax Rates
Rates apply to income between that bracket and the next highest bracket

2023 Tax Rates	Single Taxpayer	Married Filing Jointly	Married Filing Separately	Head of Household
3.10%	$0	$0	$0	$0
5.25%	$15,000	$30,000	$15,000	$15,000
5.70%	$30,000	$60,000	$30,000	$30,000

Property Tax
In Kansas, with an effective property tax rate of 1.34% and a median home value of $339,307.79, homeowners face an annual tax bill of approximately $4,552.00.

State and Local Sales Tax
Kansas imposes a 6.50% sales tax rate on most goods and services. Additionally, local jurisdictions can impose an additional 4.25% in sales tax. This brings your total potential tax rate to 10.75%. The average sales tax collection rate is around 9% in Kansas. Prescription drugs and construction materials are sales tax exempt.

Non-Resident State Income Tax
Kansas, lacking reciprocal agreements, mandates that residents working in other states and non-residents working in Kansas pay the higher of the two states' income tax rates.

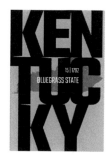

Kentucky

The Bluegrass State is one of the six states that impose an inheritance tax.

Kentucky has a special species of grazing grass that was introduced by European settlers, known as bluegrass. Through the vast amount of bluegrass pastures, Kentucky can support the thoroughbred horse industry, located in the center of the state.

In addition to Kentucky's expansive bluegrass pastures, the state levies a flat tax rate of 4.5%, which applies to both ordinary income and capital gains.

> *"Kentucky levies a flat tax rate of 4.5%, regardless of filing status or income level."*

Kentucky also offers its residents a standard deduction, which is $2,980 for all taxpayers. Married couples filing jointly can claim $5,960.

Estate and Inheritance Taxes

Although Kentucky doesn't have an estate tax, it does have an inheritance tax. But if you're a spouse, parent, child, grandchild, or sibling of the person that passed away, you're exempt. For individuals like nieces, nephews, in-laws, aunts, uncles, or great-grandchildren, there's a varying tax rate between 4% and 16%. However, there's a bit of good news: the first $1,000 of what you inherit isn't taxed. For all other beneficiaries, the rates are set between 6% and 16%, but the first $500 of your inheritance comes with no tax.

Property Tax

In Kentucky, with an effective property tax rate of 0.83% and a median home value of $245,538.86, homeowners face an annual tax bill of approximately $2,033.38.

State and Local Sales Tax

Residents of Kentucky may also need to pay sales tax at a rate of 6%. Unlike many other states, Kentucky does not allow counties to impose additional sales tax. There are a few notable exemptions to the 6% sales tax regulation, including groceries and prescription drugs.

Non-Resident State Income Tax

Kentucky, with reciprocal agreements with Illinois, Indiana, Michigan, Ohio, West Virginia, Wisconsin, and Virginia, allows residents of these states working in Kentucky, and Kentucky residents working in these states, to pay state taxes only to their respective home states.

STATE INCOME TAX

Louisiana

The Pelican State has the second-highest combined state and local sales taxes nationally.

Louisiana, nicknamed the Pelican State, celebrates the brown pelican, its state bird, both along its coastlines and on its state flag, reflecting the region's rich biodiversity and cultural heritage.

In terms of taxation, the state follows a progressive system, with rates ranging from 1.85% to 4.25%, applicable to both ordinary income and capital gains.

For 2023, individuals and those married but filing separately can claim a combined standard deduction and personal exemption of $4,500. In contrast, joint-filing couples and heads of households can claim $9,000. Furthermore, an extra $1,000 deduction is available for each dependent child on the tax return.

In addition, there are no estate or inheritance taxes in Louisiana.

Louisiana Income Tax Rates
Rates apply to income between that bracket and the next highest bracket

2023 Tax Rates	Single Taxpayer	Married Filing Jointly	Married Filing Separately	Head of Household
1.85%	$0	$0	$0	$0
3.50%	$12,500	$25,000	$12,500	$12,500
4.25%	$50,000	$100,000	$50,000	$50,000

Property Tax
In Louisiana, with an effective property tax rate of 0.56% and a median home value of $245,225.74, homeowners face an annual tax bill of approximately $1,369.03.

State and Local Sales Tax
Louisiana currently has a 4.45% sales tax rate, with a max local sales tax rate of 7%. This means that your tax on goods and services purchased can reach over 11%. Although not all counties implement local sales tax, the state's average rate on purchases is 9.46%.

Non-Resident State Income Tax
Louisiana does not have reciprocal agreements, meaning residents working in other states and non-residents working in Louisiana pay the higher of the two states' income tax rates.

STATE INCOME TAX

Maine

The Pine Tree State carries a heavy tax burden despite low combined sales taxes.

Maine, known for its majestic white pine trees, taxes residents based on a progressive rate system, with rates ranging from 5.8% to 7.15%. These rates apply to ordinary income as well as capital gains.

Despite facing large tax bills, residents can take advantage of deductions such as the 2023 personal exemption amount of $4,700 for individuals and $9,400 for married couples filing jointly.

In addition to this, Maine residents have the option to claim the federal standard deduction, which varies depending on the filing status: $13,850 for single filers or married individuals filing separately, $27,700 for married couples filing jointly, and $20,800 for heads of households.

Maine Income Tax Rates

Rates apply to income between that bracket and the next highest bracket

2023 Tax Rates	Single Taxpayer	Married Filing Jointly	Married Filing Separately	Head of Household
5.80%	$0	$0	$0	$0
6.75%	$24,500	$49,050	$24,500	$36,750
7.15%	$58,050	$116,100	$58,050	$87,100

Estate and Inheritance Taxes

In Maine, estates valued at $6,410,000 or less are exempt from the estate tax. For estates exceeding this amount, the tax rates vary between 8% and 12%. On the other hand, Maine doesn't charge any inheritance tax, which provides significant tax benefits for heirs.

Property Tax

In Maine, with an effective property tax rate of 1.24% and a median home value of $299,988.28, homeowners face an annual tax bill of approximately $3,708.68.

State and Local Sales Tax

The sales tax in Maine is currently set at 5.5%. Local sales tax collection by individual counties is not permitted. Groceries and prescription drugs are specifically exempt from sales tax.

Non-Resident State Income Tax

Maine, without reciprocal agreements, requires residents working in other states and non-residents working in Maine to pay the higher of the two states' income tax rates.

Maryland

The Old Line State is the only state to levy both an estate tax and an inheritance tax.

General George Washington is said to have coined Maryland's nickname in recognition of the Maryland Line's courageous service in numerous Revolutionary War battles.

Today, Maryland employs a progressive tax system with rates from 2.0% to 5.75% on ordinary income and capital gains.

The state offers various personal exemptions to its residents with phase-out limitations. Individual filers get a $3,200 exemption, which reduces starting at an income of $100,000 and ends entirely at $150,000. Married couples filing jointly get a $6,400 exemption, which reduces starting at an income of $150,000 and ends entirely at $200,000. Taxpayers who are blind or over the age of 65 can claim an extra $1,000. Maryland also provides a standard deduction. Individual filers can deduct $2,400, while married couples filing jointly can claim $4,850.

Maryland Income Tax Rates

Rates apply to income between that bracket and the next highest bracket

2023 Tax Rates	Single Taxpayer	Married Filing Jointly	Married Filing Separately	Head of Household
2.00%	$0	$0	$0	$0
3.00%	$1,000	$1,000	$1,000	$1,000
4.00%	$2,000	$2,000	$2,000	$2,000
4.75%	$3,000	$3,000	$3,000	$3,000
5.00%	$100,000	$150,000	$100,000	$150,000
5.25%	$125,000	$175,000	$125,000	$175,000
5.50%	$150,000	$225,000	$150,000	$225,000
5.75%	$250,000	$300,000	$250,000	$300,000

Taxpayers in Baltimore face an additional local income tax of 3.2%. Here's a breakdown of the combined local and city taxes for Baltimore residents:

Baltimore Income Tax Rates

Rates apply to income between that bracket and the next highest bracket

2023 Tax Rates	Single Taxpayer	Married Filing Jointly	Married Filing Separately	Head of Household
5.20%	$0	$0	$0	$0
6.20%	$1,000	$1,000	$1,000	$1,000
7.20%	$2,000	$2,000	$2,000	$2,000
7.95%	$3,000	$3,000	$3,000	$3,000
8.20%	$100,000	$150,000	$100,000	$150,000
8.45%	$125,000	$175,000	$125,000	$175,000
8.70%	$150,000	$225,000	$150,000	$225,000
8.95%	$250,000	$300,000	$250,000	$300,000

Estate and Inheritance Taxes

Maryland is unique in that it levies both an estate tax and an inheritance tax. For the estate tax, properties valued up to $5,000,000 are exempt, and any estate above this value is taxed between 0.8% and 16%. So, if the estate's worth is under this amount, it's free from the estate tax. When it comes to the inheritance tax, close family members, like spouses, children, parents, grandparents, stepparents, and siblings are exempt. However, other heirs face a 10% tax on their inheritance.

Property Tax

In Maryland, with an effective property tax rate of 1.05% and a median home value of $385,548.86, homeowners face an annual tax bill of approximately $4,042.66.

State and Local Sales Tax

Sales tax is assessed at a rate of 6% in Maryland. Maryland does not permit counties to levy additional local taxes on top of the state mandated rate. Unlike many other states, Maryland assesses this sales tax on groceries and other commodities. However, agricultural products are specifically excluded from sales tax.

Non-Resident State Income Tax

Maryland's reciprocal agreements with the District of Columbia, Pennsylvania, Virginia, and West Virginia enable residents of these areas working in Maryland, and Maryland residents working in these areas, to pay state taxes only to their respective home states.

Massachusetts

The Bay State's millionaire's tax raises the top rate to 9%, one of the highest in the nation.

Known for iconic Cape Cod, Massachusetts also has a distinct income tax system.

Starting in 2023, incomes up to $1 million will be taxed at 5%, while anything over that threshold faces a 9% tax,

Though residents can't apply the federal standard deduction to their state returns, they can claim a personal exemption: $4,400 for single filers or married individuals filing separately, $6,800 for heads of households, and $8,800 for married couples filing jointly. Additionally, an extra $1,000 exemption is available per dependent child.

Massachusetts Income Tax

Rates apply to income between each bracket and the next higher bracket

2023 Tax Rates	Tax Bracket
5.00%	$0
9.00%	$1,000,000

Capital Gains Tax

Massachusetts applies a flat tax rate of 5% on both ordinary income and most long-term capital gains. However, specific capital gains, such as short-term capital gains and long-term capital gains on collectibles and pre-1996 installment sales, are taxed at a higher rate of 12%.

Estate and Inheritance Taxes

In Massachusetts, estates valued at $2,000,000 or less are exempt from estate tax. For those exceeding this amount, the tax rates vary between 0.8% and 16%. On the other hand, Massachusetts doesn't have an inheritance tax.

Property Tax

In Massachusetts, with an effective property tax rate of 1.14% and a median home value of $554,204.65, homeowners face an annual tax bill of approximately $6,312.64.

State and Local Sales Tax

In Massachusetts, there is a 6.25% sales and use tax that applies to most tangible products and certain services sold to consumers. However, some essential items like food, clothing, and prescriptions, are exempt from this tax, along with most services and certain things used in manufacturing businesses. Local jurisdictions are not allowed to impose a local sales tax.

Non-Resident State Income Tax

Massachusetts, without reciprocal agreements, requires residents working in other states and non-residents working in Massachusetts to pay the higher of the two states' income tax rates.

STATE INCOME TAX

Michigan

The Great Lake State reduced its flat income tax rate from 4.25% to 4.05% this year.

Michigan's nickname comes from the state's unique geographical feature of being bordered by four of the five Great Lakes in North America.

Michigan has a flat tax rate of 4.05%, which applies to ordinary income as well as capital gains. In Detroit, residents face an additional local income tax of 2.4%

Every taxpayer and their dependents can claim a personal exemption of $5,000. This means a single filer can deduct $5,000, while a married couple filing together can deduct $10,000. For those over 67, Michigan offers a generous standard deduction on retirement and pension income: $20,000 for singles and those married but filing separately, and $40,000 for joint-filing couples.

Also, Michigan residents don't have to worry about estate or inheritance taxes, as the state doesn't impose them.

"Detroit residents pay a combined state and local income tax of 6.45%."

Property Tax

In Michigan, with an effective property tax rate of 1.38% and a median home value of $227,563.06, homeowners face an annual tax bill of approximately $3,136.39.

State and Local Sales Tax

Michigan charges a 6% state sales tax on most purchases. Certain items, such as natural gas, electricity, and other home heating fuels are taxed at a lower rate of 4%. Michigan does not have any provisions that allow counties to charge local sales tax.

Non-Resident State Income Tax

Michigan has reciprocal agreements with Wisconsin, Indiana, Kentucky, Illinois, Ohio, and Minnesota, allowing residents of these states working in Michigan, and Michigan residents working in these states, to pay state taxes only to their respective home states.

STATE INCOME TAX

Minnesota

The Land of 10,000 Lakes has the eighth-highest overall tax burden in the nation.

Minnesota's nickname was coined by early settlers to showcase the state's numerous lakes and attract more people.

Contrasting with this natural appeal, the state is known for its high tax rates, including a top bracket of 9.85% on ordinary income and capital gains.

Minnesota residents can reduce taxable income in 2023 through standard deductions and dependent exemptions. Individuals can claim a $13,825 deduction that phases out between $110,325 and $1 million. Heads of households have a $20,800 deduction phasing out from $165,986 to $1 million. Married couples filing jointly can deduct $27,650, with phase-out beginning at $220,650 and ending at $1 million. Additionally, taxpayers can claim a $4,800 exemption for each dependent.

Minnesota Income Tax Rates
Rates apply to income between that bracket and the next highest bracket

2023 Tax Rates	Single Taxpayer	Married Filing Jointly	Married Filing Separately	Head of Household
5.35%	$0	$0	$0	$0
6.80%	$30,070	$43,950	$21,975	$37,010
7.85%	$98,760	$174,610	$87,305	$148,730
9.85%	$183,340	$304,970	$152,485	$243,720

Estate and Inheritance Taxes

In Minnesota, estates valued at $3,000,000 or less are exempt from estate tax. For those exceeding this amount, the tax rates vary between 13% and 16%. However, Minnesota doesn't have an inheritance tax, which means heirs can benefit from significant tax savings.

Property Tax

In Minnesota, with an effective property tax rate of 1.11% and a median home value of $324,993.23, homeowners face an annual tax bill of approximately $3,598.65.

State and Local Sales Tax

Minnesota has a state sales tax rate of 6.875%. In addition, local jurisdictions can assess an extra tax of up to 2.0%. Many counties do not impose these additional taxes. However, counties, like Hermantown City and Carlton County, max out the 2.0%.

Non-Resident State Income Tax

Minnesota's reciprocal agreements with Michigan and North Dakota mean residents of these states working in Minnesota, and Minnesota residents working in these states, pay state taxes only to their respective home states.

Mississippi

The Magnolia State has low property tax rates but high sales taxes compared to other states.

Mississippi earns its nickname from the abundant magnolia trees gracing its picturesque landscape.

Beyond its scenic beauty, Mississippi has a flat individual income tax rate of 5%, which applies to ordinary income as well as capital gains.

The state offers a standard deduction of $2,300 for individual filers, $3,400 for heads of households, and $4,600 for married couples filing jointly.

> *"Mississippi levies a flat tax rate of 5%, on income exceeding $10,0000, regardless of filing status."*

Residents also can claim personal exemptions based on filing status: $6,000 for individual filers, $8,000 for heads of households, and $12,000 for married couples filing jointly. Each dependent adds an extra $1,500 exemption. Taxpayers over 65 or those who are blind can claim an additional $1,500.

In addition, the state doesn't have estate or inheritance taxes.

Property Tax

In Mississippi, with an effective property tax rate of 0.67% and a median home value of $251,271.58, homeowners face an annual tax bill of approximately $1,681.28.

State and Local Sales Tax

Mississippi has a state sales tax rate of 7%, with a combined state and local tax rate cap of 8%. Clothing, groceries, prescription drugs, and over-the-counter drugs are all subject to sales tax. Vending machine sales, janitorial services, and transportation services are excluded.

Non-Resident State Income Tax

Mississippi residents working in other states and non-residents working in Mississippi pay the higher of the two states' income tax rates, as there are no reciprocal agreements.

STATE INCOME TAX

Missouri

The Show Me State's top tax rate is low, but most taxpayers still fall into the highest bracket.

Missouri's nickname is widely attributed to an 1899 speech by U.S. Congressman Willard Duncan Vandiver. His phrase, "I'm from Missouri, and you've got to show me," showcased his skepticism and came to symbolize the straightforward nature of the state's residents.

The state uses a progressive tax system, with rates ranging from 2% to 4.95%, which apply to ordinary income as well as capital gains.

Missouri allows residents to use the federal standard deduction on state returns: $13,850 for single filers and married individuals filing separately, $20,800 for heads of households, and $27,700 for married couples filing jointly.

The state doesn't offer additional personal exemptions. However, Missouri has provisions that benefit retirees, with married couples filing jointly able to exclude Social Security payments from taxable income if their adjusted gross income is under $100,000. This threshold is reduced to $85,000 for single taxpayers.

Missouri Income Tax Rate

Rates apply to income between each
bracket and the next higher bracket

2023 Tax Rates	Tax Bracket
0.00%	$0
2.00%	$1,207
2.50%	$2,414
3.00%	$3,621
3.50%	$4,828
4.00%	$6,035
4.50%	$7,242
4.95%	$8,449

On another positive note, the state doesn't have estate or inheritance taxes.

Property Tax

In Missouri, with an effective property tax rate of 1.01% and a median home value of $239,939.24, homeowners face an annual tax bill of approximately $2,418.15.

State and Local Sales Tax

Missouri assesses a 4.225% state sales tax rate. Counties can add another 5.88% in local taxes. This brings your potential sales tax rate to over 10%. However, groceries are subject to a lower state tax rate of 1.225%, while prescription drugs are exempt. These stiff sales tax rates can make living in Missouri more expensive.

Non-Resident State Income Tax

Missouri, not having reciprocal agreements, means both residents working in other states and non-residents working in Missouri are subject to the higher of the two states' tax rates.

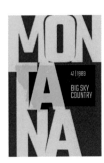

STATE INCOME TAX

Montana

The Big Sky Country has a low tax burden, thanks to no sales taxes and low property tax rates.

Nicknamed "Big Sky Country" for its expansive and seemingly endless skies, Montana's landscape offers a sense of vastness and freedom. This term, popularized by A.B. Guthrie Jr.'s novel *The Big Sky,* aptly describes the state's open, panoramic vistas.

Alongside this natural grandeur, Montana operates a progressive tax system, with rates varying from 1% to 6.75%.

Residents can deduct 20% of their adjusted gross income, with a cap of $5,540 for individual filers and those married filing separately. For heads of households and married couples filing jointly, the limit is $11,080.

Additionally, there's a personal exemption of $2,960 for each taxpayer and qualifying dependent. This means married couples filing together can claim a combined exemption of $5,920.

Montana Income Tax Rates

Rates apply to income between each bracket and the next higher bracket

2023 Tax Rates	Tax Bracket
1.00%	$0
2.00%	$3,600
3.00%	$6,300
4.00%	$9,700
5.00%	$13,000
6.00%	$16,800
6.75%	$21,600

Capital Gains Tax

Montana taxes capital gains at the same rates as ordinary income, but it has a 2% capital gains credit. This means taxpayers can claim an income tax credit of up to 2% of their net capital gains.

Property Tax

In Montana, with an effective property tax rate of 0.74% and a median home value of $453,898.47, homeowners face an annual tax bill of approximately $3,352.93.

State and Local Sales Tax

Montana is one of the few states that does not charge state or local sales tax. However, you may have to pay a sales tax on lodging and car rentals.

Non-Resident State Income Tax

Montana's reciprocal agreement with North Dakota allows residents of Montana working in North Dakota, and North Dakota residents working in Montana, to pay state taxes only to their respective home states.

STATE INCOME TAX

Nebraska

The Cornhusker State's income and property tax rates are higher than its neighboring states.

Nebraska, known for its history of hand-husking corn before machines, now stands out for its tax system. Residents quickly hit the highest tax bracket of 6.64%, which applies to ordinary income as well as capital gains.

But Nebraska offers a standard deduction of $7,900 for individuals, $15,800 for married couples filing jointly, and $11,600 for heads of households.

On top of that, you can get a credit of $157 for each Nebraska personal exemption claimed in the 2023 tax year.

Nebraska Income Tax Rates
Rates apply to income between that bracket and the next highest bracket

2023 Tax Rates	Single Taxpayer	Married Filing Jointly	Married Filing Separately	Head of Household
2.46%	$0	$0	$0	$0
3.51%	$3,700	$7,390	$3,700	$6,900
5.01%	$22,170	$44,350	$22,170	$35,480
6.64%	$35,720	$71,460	$35,730	$52,980

Estate and Inheritance Taxes

While Nebraska doesn't levy an estate tax, it does impose an inheritance tax. Spouses are completely exempt from this tax, as are transfers to individuals younger than 21 or to organizations focused on religious, charitable, public, scientific, or educational objectives.

Transfers to immediate family members, other than spouses, are taxed at 1%, but each beneficiary has an exemption up to $100,000. Distant relatives are taxed at 11% with a $40,000 exemption per beneficiary. For individuals not related, the tax rate is 15%, with a $25,000 exemption for each beneficiary.

Property Tax

In Nebraska, with an effective property tax rate of 1.63% and a median home value of $295,131.24, homeowners face an annual tax bill of approximately $4,818.74.

State and Local Sales Tax

Nebraska imposes both state and local sales tax. The state tax rate is 5.5%, with a maximum local rate of 2%. However, Nebraska is decreasing the maximum local rate to 1.5% beginning on October 1, 2023. Nebraska has a lengthy list of sales tax exemptions including laundromats, newspapers, energy, food, lodging, and telecommunications.

Non-Resident State Income Tax

Nebraska, lacking reciprocal agreements, requires residents working elsewhere and non-residents in Nebraska to pay the higher of the two states' tax rates.

STATE INCOME TAX

Nevada

The Silver State levies no state income tax but has relatively high sales taxes.

Nevada, recognized for the silver boom that began in 1859 and the iconic Las Vegas Strip, also provides financial advantages to its residents. The state doesn't impose taxes on personal income, capital gains, estates, or inheritances.

"Nevada does not have a state income tax."

Property Tax

In Nevada, with an effective property tax rate of 0.59% and a median home value of $399,719.53, homeowners face an annual tax bill of approximately $2,355.66.

State and Local Sales Tax

The base sales tax in Nevada is set at 6.85%. However, counties can levy additional taxes, causing the total sales tax rate to fluctuate between 6.85% and 8.375%, depending on the county. Groceries, medical devices, and prescription drugs are exempt from sales tax.

Non-Resident State Income Tax

Nevada has no state income tax. Nevada residents working in other states pay income taxes to those states. Non-residents working in Nevada pay income taxes to their own states.

STATE INCOME TAX

New Hampshire

The Granite State only taxes income from dividends and interest.

New Hampshire, with its stunning granite formations, has a flat income tax of 4% that applies to dividends and interest income only. The state doesn't tax wages, sales, capital gains, inheritances, or estates.

"New Hampshire levies a flat tax rate of 4% on dividends and interest income only."

In addition, taxpayers can take advantage of a $2,400 exemption from this tax, providing some relief for their tax liabilities. Additionally, individuals aged 65 or older, as well as those who are blind, can claim an extra $1,200 exemption, while those under 65 and unable to work due to disability also receive the same $1,200 exemption.

Property Tax
In New Hampshire, with an effective property tax rate of 1.93% and a median home value of $398,886.09, homeowners face an annual tax bill of approximately $7,698.34.

State and Local Sales Tax
There is no state or local sales tax assessed on general purchases in New Hampshire. However, there are excise taxes levied on alcohol, tobacco, cigarettes, and gasoline.

Non-Resident State Income Tax
New Hampshire only taxes interest and dividends. New Hampshire residents working in other states pay income taxes to those states. Non-residents working in New Hampshire pay income taxes to their own states on wage income.

New Jersey

The Garden State's income tax and property tax rates are among the highest in the country.

New Jersey, originally nicknamed for its abundant garden landscapes, has since evolved into a symbol of industrialization and progress.

However, this transformation has also introduced a complex fiscal landscape for its residents, characterized by high tax brackets that reach rates of up to 10.75%, which apply to ordinary income as well as capital gains. Residents of Newark pay an additional local tax on earned income of 1%.

> *"Newark residents pay a 1% local income tax in addition to the state income tax."*

New Jersey offers a personal exemption of $1,000 to assist taxpayers in reducing their taxable income, a figure that doubles to $2,000 for married couples filing jointly. For honorably discharged veterans, an increased personal exemption of $6,000 is available. Furthermore, each dependent allows for an added personal exemption of $1,500.

New Jersey Income Tax Rates
Rates apply to income between that bracket and the next highest bracket

2023 Tax Rates	Single Taxpayer	Married Filing Jointly	Married Filing Separately	Head of Household
1.40%	$0	$0	$0	$0
1.75%	$20,000	$20,000	$20,000	$20,000
2.45%	$35,000	$50,000	$35,000	$50,000
3.50%	na	$70,000	na	$70,000
5.53%	$40,000	$80,000	$40,000	$80,000
6.37%	$75,000	$150,000	$75,000	$150,000
8.97%	$500,000	$500,000	$500,000	$500,000
10.75%	$1,000,000	$1,000,000	$1,000,000	$1,000,000

Estate and Inheritance Taxes

While New Jersey doesn't levy an estate tax, it does impose an inheritance tax. The inheritance tax is all about your relationship to the person who passed away and the amount you inherit. If you're close relatives, like spouses, kids, or grandparents — you are exempt from inheritance tax. For other relatives like siblings or your child's spouse, the first $25,000 you inherit isn't taxed. After that, rates vary from 11% to 16%, depending on how much you inherit. And for everyone else, the tax rate starts at 15% for inheritances up to $700,000, and if it's over that, it bumps up to 16%.

Property Tax

In New Jersey, with an effective property tax rate of 2.23% and a median home value of $425,019.13, homeowners face an annual tax bill of approximately $9,498.79.

State and Local Sales Tax

New Jersey assesses a 6.625% sales tax on goods and services. There is no local sales tax, but in Urban Enterprise Zones — such as Newark, Jersey City, Elizabeth, and Trenton, to name a few — qualified retailers are permitted to charge an additional sales tax of 3.31%. Groceries, household paper products, and prescription drugs are exempt from sales tax. Furthermore, New Jersey drivers pay an additional 41.4 cents per gallon on gas.

Non-Resident State Income Tax

New Jersey's reciprocal agreement with Pennsylvania permits residents of New Jersey working in Pennsylvania, and Pennsylvania residents working in New Jersey, to pay state taxes only to their respective home states.

STATE INCOME TAX

New Mexico

The Land of Enchantment has low property taxes and an average top marginal tax rate.

New Mexico, with its beautiful landscape earning it the nickname the Land of Enchantment, has a progressive tax structure for its residents, with rates ranging from 1.7% to 5.9%.

New Mexico taxpayers can benefit from the federal standard deduction, which reduces taxable income by $13,850 for single filers and married individuals filing separately, $20,800 for heads of households, and $27,700 for married couples filing jointly.

For those with dependents, the state offers a deduction of $4,000 per dependent, except for one. If you are on active duty in the military, all your income is tax-exempt.

On another positive note, New Mexico doesn't have estate or inheritance taxes.

New Mexico Income Tax Rates
Rates apply to income between that bracket and the next highest bracket

2023 Tax Rates	Single Taxpayer	Married Filing Jointly	Married Filing Separately	Head of Household
1.70%	$0	$0	$0	$0
3.20%	$5,500	$8,000	$4,000	$8,000
4.70%	$11,000	$16,000	$8,000	$16,000
4.90%	$16,000	$24,000	$12,000	$24,000
5.90%	$210,000	$315,000	$157,500	$315,000

Capital Gains Tax
New Mexico taxes capital gains at the same rates as ordinary income. However, the state allows filers to deduct either 40% of capital gains income or $1,000, whichever is greater.

Property Tax

In New Mexico, with an effective property tax rate of 0.67% and a median home value of $329,815.54, homeowners face an annual tax bill of approximately $2,215.33.

State and Local Sales Tax

While New Mexico doesn't impose a traditional sales tax, it does levy a gross receipts tax on businesses at a rate of 4.875%. Local jurisdictions may add up to an additional 4.0625%. Typically, businesses pass this cost onto consumers, effectively making it a kind of sales tax.

Non-Resident State Income Tax

New Mexico residents and non-residents working in the state face the higher of the two states' tax rates due to the absence of reciprocal agreements.

STATE INCOME TAX

New York

The Empire State's high taxes, especially in New York City, are among the highest in the country.

New York, famously known as the Empire State for its wealth and influence, a nickname credited to George Washington, also stands out for its tax policies.

The state has a progressive tax system with rates from 4% to 10.9%. In New York City, residents face additional income taxes, ranging from 3.08% to 3.88%. Both the state and the city apply these rates to ordinary income and capital gains.

For the tax year 2023, New York state offers the following standard deductions: $8,000 for single taxpayers and married individuals filing separately, $16,050 for married couples filing jointly, and $11,200 for heads of households. Also, New York residents can claim a $1,000 exemption for each eligible dependent, which can further reduce their taxable income.

New York State Income Tax Rates
Rates apply to income between that bracket and the next highest bracket

2023 Tax Rates	Single Taxpayer	Married Filing Jointly	Married Filing Separately	Head of Household
4.00%	$0	$0	$0	$0
4.50%	$8,500	$17,150	$8,500	$12,800
5.25%	$11,700	$23,600	$11,700	$17,650
5.50%	$13,900	$27,900	$13,900	$20,900
6.00%	$80,650	$161,550	$80,650	$107,650
6.85%	$215,400	$323,200	$215,400	$269,300
9.65%	$1,077,550	$2,155,350	$1,077,550	$1,616,450
10.30%	$5,000,000	$5,000,000	$5,000,000	$5,000,000
10.90%	$25,000,000	$25,000,000	$25,000,000	$25,000,000

Residents of all five boroughs — Manhattan, Brooklyn, Queens, The Bronx, and Staten Island — are subject to the New York City local income tax.

Here are the combined state and local tax rates for New York City residents:

New York City Income Tax Rates

Rates apply to income between that bracket and the next highest bracket

2023 Tax Rates	Single Taxpayer	Married Filing Jointly	Married Filing Separately	Head of Household
7.08%	$0	$0	$0	$0
7.58%	$8,500	$17,150	$8,500	$12,800
8.33%	$11,700	$23,600	$11,700	$17,650
9.01%	$13,900	$27,900	$13,900	$20,900
9.07%	$25,000	$45,000	$25,000	$30,000
9.38%	$50,000	$90,000	$50,000	$60,000
9.88%	$80,650	$161,550	$80,650	$107,650
10.73%	$215,400	$323,200	$215,400	$269,300
13.53%	$1,077,550	$2,155,350	$1,077,550	$1,616,450
14.18%	$5,000,000	$5,000,000	$5,000,000	$5,000,000
14.78%	$25,000,000	$25,000,000	$25,000,000	$25,000,000

Estate and Inheritance Taxes

Although New York doesn't have an inheritance tax, the state charges an estate tax that ranges from 3.06% to 16%.

The way New York calculates its estate tax is unique and different from the federal approach. The rule of thumb is, if you leave assets to someone other than your spouse or a charity and it's under $6,580,000 in 2023, you won't have to pay any New York estate tax.

However, this tax break starts to fade once you pass that limit. In fact, if the estate's value goes beyond the limit by more than 5% (which is $6,909,000 for 2023), the entire value of the estate becomes taxable. This steep drop-off is why it's sometimes referred to as a "cliff tax." If your estate's value lies between the threshold amount and the 5% excess, a portion of it will face the New York estate tax.

Property Tax

In New York, with an effective property tax rate of 1.40% and a median home value of $449,924.05, homeowners face an annual tax bill of approximately $6,306.13.

State and Local Sales Tax

New York assesses a 4% sales tax on most goods and services. Counties can charge a local tax rate of up to 4.875%, making the total combined rate 8.875%. Residents of New York can expect to pay around 8% on purchases, with jurisdictions like the Bronx, Kings, Manhattan, and Queens maxing out the rate.

Non-Resident State Income Tax

New York, without reciprocal agreements, requires residents working in other states and non-residents working in New York to pay the higher of the two states' tax rates.

North Carolina

The Old North State has higher taxes than all its neighboring states, except Virginia.

After Carolina's split in 1710, the older northern region became North Carolina, earning the nickname Old North State.

Today, its residents enjoy a uniform tax rate of 4.75% on both ordinary income and capital gains. The state's flat tax rate is anticipated to decline over the next five years, ultimately reaching a rate of 3.99% by 2027, potentially providing further tax relief for its residents.

> *"North Carolina levies a flat income tax rate of 4.75%, regardless of income or filing status."*

North Carolina does not have a personal exemption for its residents, but it does offer taxpayers a standard deduction to lower taxable income: $12,750 for single filers and married individuals filing separately, $25,500 for married couples filing jointly, and $19,125 for heads of households.

North Carolina does not have estate or inheritance taxes.

Property Tax

In North Carolina, with an effective property tax rate of 0.82% and a median home value of $324,992.86, homeowners face an annual tax bill of approximately $2,650.30.

State and Local Sales Tax

The state sales tax rate in North Carolina is 4.75%. Counties in North Carolina can impose additional local taxes, up to a combined rate of 7.5%. The average state and local sales tax rate you can expect to pay is around 7%.

Non-Resident State Income Tax

North Carolina does not have reciprocal agreements, so residents and non-residents are subject to the higher tax rate of either North Carolina or their home or work state.

STATE INCOME TAX

North Dakota

The Peace Garden State's low income tax rates contribute to the state's affordable cost of living.

The International Peace Garden, straddling the border of North Dakota and Canada, symbolizes a lasting pledge between the US and Canada to maintain peaceful relations, giving rise to the state's nickname.

North Dakota stands out not just for its iconic garden but also for its recent tax revisions. The state eliminated two of its five tax brackets and made retroactive rate adjustments, leading to many being exempted from taxation. The current tax rates vary from 0% to 2.5%.

Residents of North Dakota can take the federal standard deduction: $13,850 for single filers and married individuals filing separately, $20,800 for heads of households, and $27,700 for married couples filing jointly.

Another advantage is that North Dakota does not impose estate or inheritance taxes.

North Dakota Income Tax Rates
Rates apply to income between that bracket and the next highest bracket

2023 Tax Rates	Single Taxpayer	Married Filing Jointly	Married Filing Separately	Head of Household
0.00%	$0	$0	$0	$0
1.95%	$44,725	$74,750	$37,375	$59,950
2.50%	$225,975	$275,100	$137,550	$250,550

Capital Gains Tax
North Dakota taxes capital gains at the same rates as ordinary income. However, the state allows filers to deduct 40% of capital gains income.

Property Tax
In North Dakota, with an effective property tax rate of 0.98% and a median home value of $290,205.71, homeowners face an annual tax bill of approximately $2,840.36.

State and Local Sales Tax

North Dakota has a state sales tax rate of 5%, with localities able to assess an additional 3.5% in taxes. The average combined rate in North Dakota is around 7%. There are some tax-exempt items, including groceries and prescription drugs. Diapers became sales tax-exempt beginning on July 1, 2023.

Non-Resident State Income Tax

North Dakota, with reciprocal agreements with Minnesota and Montana, enables residents of these states working in North Dakota, and North Dakota residents working in these states, to pay state taxes only to their respective home states.

STATE INCOME TAX

Ohio

The Buckeye State has relatively low income tax rates, but above-average property tax rates.

Known as the Buckeye State due to its abundance of buckeye trees, Ohio also stands out economically. It uses a single tax bracket for all filing statuses with rates ranging from 2.75% to 3.75%, which apply to ordinary income as well as capital gains.

To alleviate tax burdens, taxpayers with an income of $40,000 or below can claim personal exemptions of $4,800 for married couples filing jointly, and $2,400 for individual taxpayers.

Additionally, an exemption of $2,400 can be claimed for each dependent. However, as income levels rise, these exemption amounts are subject to a slight reduction.

Another advantage is that Ohio does not impose estate or inheritance taxes.

Ohio Income Tax Rate

Rates apply to income between each bracket and the next higher bracket

2023 Tax Rates	Tax Bracket
0.00%	$0
2.75%	$26,050
3.69%	$100,000
3.75%	$115,300

Property Tax

In Ohio, with an effective property tax rate of 1.59% and a median home value of $219,903.20, homeowners face an annual tax bill of approximately $3,499.09.

State and Local Sales Tax

Ohio assesses a state sales tax rate of 5.75%. Local taxes are also allowed up to 2.25%. This brings your potential combined sales tax rate to 8%. Like many states, prescription drugs and groceries are sales tax-exempt. Gas and diesel are subject to an added tax of 38.5 and 47 cents per gallon, respectively.

Non-Resident State Income Tax

Ohio's reciprocal agreements with Indiana, Kentucky, Michigan, Pennsylvania, and West Virginia allow residents of these states working in Ohio, and Ohio residents working in these states, to pay state taxes only to their respective home states.

STATE INCOME TAX

Oklahoma

The Sooner State offers relatively low income taxes rates as well as capital gains deductions.

As pioneers eagerly settled in Oklahoma for its fertile farming land, their energetic and can-do attitudes earned them the nickname "sooners."

Fast forward to the present, Oklahoma uses a progressive tax system, with rates ranging from 0.25% to 4.75%.

The state provides its residents with a $1,000 personal exemption, which doubles to $2,000 for married couples filing jointly, while each dependent adds an additional $1,000 exemption. Single filers and married individuals filing separately can take a $6,350 standard deduction, heads of households can claim $9,350, and married couples filing jointly can claim $12,700.

Another benefit is that Oklahoma does not levy taxes on estates or inheritances.

Oklahoma Income Tax Rates

Rates apply to income between that bracket and the next highest bracket

2023 Tax Rates	Single Taxpayer	Married Filing Jointly	Married Filing Separately	Head of Household
0.25%	$0	$0	$0	$0
0.75%	$1,000	$2,000	$1,000	$2,000
1.75%	$2,500	$5,000	$2,500	$5,000
2.75%	$3,750	$7,500	$3,750	$7,500
3.75%	$4,900	$9,800	$4,900	$9,800
4.75%	$7,200	$12,200	$7,200	$12,200

Capital Gains Tax

Oklahoma treats capital gains the same way as ordinary income when it comes to taxation. However, you get a full deduction on capital gains from selling Oklahoma property you've owned for at least five continuous years. Similarly, if you sell shares or ownership stakes in an Oklahoma-based company, LLC, or partnership held for a minimum of two continuous years, those gains are also fully deductible.

Property Tax

In Oklahoma, with an effective property tax rate of 0.89% and a median home value of $233,547.78, homeowners face an annual tax bill of approximately $2,083.89.

State and Local Sales Tax

Oklahoma is one of the few states that allow municipalities to levy significant sales tax in addition to the 4.5% state rate. The maximum state and local rate in Oklahoma is 11.5%. This means that on a $100 purchase, you could be paying nearly $12 in sales tax.

Non-Resident State Income Tax

Oklahoma residents and non-residents working in the state are subject to the higher of the two states' tax rates, as there are no reciprocal agreements.

STATE INCOME TAX

Oregon

High earners in the Beaver State, particularly in Portland, face high income tax rates.

From its rich history with beaver fur trading, which earned it the nickname, to its captivating landscapes and abundant wildlife today, Oregon has much to offer.

On the tax front, the state uses a progressive tax system with rates ranging from 4.75% to 9.9%, which apply to ordinary income as well as capital gains.

Residents enjoy the perks of a personal exemption and standard deduction. In 2023, the standard deduction is $2,605 for single filers and married individuals filing separately, $4,195 for heads of households, and $5,210 for married couples filing jointly. The personal exemption credit amounts to $236 for individual taxpayers and each eligible dependent, while married couples filing jointly can claim $472.

Oregon Income Tax Rates
Rates apply to income between that bracket and the next highest bracket

2023 Tax Rates	Single Taxpayer	Married Filing Jointly	Married Filing Separately	Head of Household
4.75%	$0	$0	$0	$0
6.75%	$4,050	$8,100	$4,050	$8,100
8.75%	$10,200	$20,400	$10,200	$20,400
9.90%	$125,000	$250,000	$125,000	$250,000

In Portland, residents are subject to an additional 1% Metro tax on income over $125,000 for individuals and $200,000 for joint filers. On top of that, residents of Multnomah County face the Preschool for All personal income tax, ranging from 1.5% to 3.0% based on income and filing status. So, if you live in Portland, within Multnomah County, your total tax liability will include these local taxes on top of the state and federal taxes.

Here's a breakdown of the combined state and local taxes for Portland residents in Multnomah County:

Portland Income Tax Rates

Rates apply to income between that bracket and the next highest bracket

2023 Tax Rates	Single Taxpayer	Married Filing Jointly	Married Filing Separately	Head of Household
Single Taxpayers and Married Filing Separately				
4.75%	$0	na	$0	na
6.75%	$4,050	na	$4,050	na
8.75%	$10,200	na	$10,200	na
12.40%	$125,000	na	$125,000	na
13.90%	$250,000	na	$250,000	na
Married Filing Jointly and Head of Household				
4.75%	na	$0	na	$0
6.75%	na	$8,100	na	$8,100
8.75%	na	$20,400	na	$20,400
10.25%	na	$200,000	na	$200,000
12.40%	na	$250,000	na	$250,000
13.90%	na	$400,000	na	$400,000

Estate and Inheritance Taxes

In Oregon, estates valued at $1,000,000 or less are exempt from estate tax. For those exceeding this amount, the tax rates vary between 10% and 16%. However, Oregon doesn't have an inheritance tax, which means heirs can benefit from significant tax savings.

Property Tax

In Oregon, with an effective property tax rate of 0.93% and a median home value of $474,997.25, homeowners face an annual tax bill of approximately $4,427.21.

State and Local Sales Tax

Oregon does not currently have a state sales tax. However, Oregon does impose a gross receipts tax of between 6.6% and 7.6% on corporate income.

Non-Resident State Income Tax

Oregon, lacking reciprocal agreements, requires residents working in other states and non-residents working in Oregon to pay the higher of the two states' tax rates.

STATE INCOME TAX

Pennsylvania

The Keystone State imposes relatively high property taxes as well as an inheritance tax.

Pennsylvania, nicknamed the Keystone State for its fundamental role in founding the United States, offers its residents a flat tax rate of 3.07%, which applies to ordinary income as well as capital gains. Philadelphia residents pay an additional income tax of 3.87%.

Unlike many other states, Pennsylvania does not allow its taxpayers to claim a personal exemption or a standard deduction.

"Philadelphia residents pay a combined state and local income tax of 6.94%."

Estate and Inheritance Taxes

Although Pennsylvania doesn't have an estate tax, it does have an inheritance tax. When you inherit from a direct family member, such as your child or parent, you're looking at a 4.5% tax. If what you're inheriting is from a sibling, then the tax goes up a bit to 12%. For all other heirs, the tax stands at 15%. However, for spouses who share ownership of a property, there's no inheritance tax on that. Also, inheriting from your spouse or, for parents, from a child 21 or younger, means no tax either.

Property Tax

In Pennsylvania, with an effective property tax rate of 1.49% and a median home value of $275,004.41, homeowners face an annual tax bill of approximately $4,097.96.

State and Local Sales Tax

Pennsylvania has a 6% state sales tax rate, which is high compared to many other states. However, the local sales tax rate is capped at 2%. The combined state and local sales tax rate comes out to around 6.34%.

Non-Resident State Income Tax

Pennsylvania, with reciprocal agreements with Indiana, Maryland, New Jersey, Ohio, Virginia, and West Virginia, ensures residents of these states working in Pennsylvania, and Pennsylvania residents working in these states, pay state taxes only to their respective home states.

STATE INCOME TAX

Rhode Island

The Ocean State has the eleventh-highest overall tax burden in the nation.

Rhode Island offers its residents breathtaking views of the ocean, with over 400 miles of coastline packed into the small state.

It uses a graduated tax system, with rates ranging from 3.75% to 5.99%, which apply to ordinary income as well as capital gains.

Rhode Island residents enjoy their fair share of tax breaks, with the ability to claim both a standard deduction and personal exemption.

The 2023 standard deduction is $10,000 for single filers, $10,025 for married individuals filing separately, $15,050 for heads of households, and $20,050 for married couples filing jointly.

The state offers its residents a $4,700 personal exemption for each taxpayer and eligible dependent. This means that married couples filing jointly can claim up to $9,400. The personal exemption does begin to phase out at an adjusted gross income of $233,750, with a complete phaseout once the adjusted gross income reaches $260,550. These figures are doubled for married couples filing jointly.

Rhode Island Income Tax

Rates apply to income between each bracket and the next higher bracket

2023 Tax Rates	Tax Bracket
3.75%	$0
4.75%	$73,450
5.99%	$166,950

Estate and Inheritance Taxes
In Rhode Island, the estate tax rates range from 0.8% to 16%. However, if an estate's value is $1,733,264 or less, it's exempt from this tax. Therefore, estates below this value won't be subject to the estate tax. Rhode Island does not levy an inheritance tax, offering notable tax savings for heirs.

Property Tax

In Rhode Island, with an effective property tax rate of 1.40% and a median home value of $406,540.00, homeowners face an annual tax bill of approximately $5,684.58.

State and Local Sales Tax

Rhode Island's sales tax rate is relatively high at 7%; however, local counties are not allowed to assess an additional sales tax rate. Printed books, fuel oil, and clothing are exempt from state sales tax.

Non-Resident State Income Tax

Rhode Island, without reciprocal agreements, means both residents working in other states and non-residents working in Rhode Island pay the higher of the two states' tax rates.

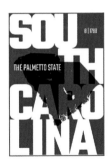

STATE INCOME TAX

South Carolina

The Palmetto State offers reduced income tax rates for taxpayers in the highest bracket this year.

South Carolina gets its nickname from the vast population of Sabal Palmetto trees.

Residents of South Carolina also enjoy a top tax bracket rate cut from 7% to 6.5% in the 2023 tax year. In addition, Social Security benefits are excluded from taxation, which makes the state appealing to retirees.

The standard deductions for South Carolina correspond with federal standard deductions, $13,800 for single filers and married individuals filing separately, $20,800 for heads of households, and $27,700 for married couples filing jointly. South Carolina also provides a $4,430 exemption for each eligible dependent.

Another positive aspect to note is that South Carolina does not impose estate or inheritance taxes.

South Carolina Income Tax

Rates apply to income between each bracket and the next higher bracket

2023 Tax Rates	Tax Bracket
0.00%	$0
3.00%	$3,200
6.50%	$16,040

Capital Gains Tax

South Carolina taxes capital gains at the same rates as ordinary income. On long-term capital gains, taxpayers are allowed a deduction of 44%.

Property Tax

In South Carolina, with an effective property tax rate of 0.57% and a median home value of $329,820.86, homeowners face an annual tax bill of approximately $1,869.42.

State and Local Sales Tax

South Carolina imposes a state sales tax rate of 6%. Counties also have the ability to impose an additional tax of 3%, making the maximum state and local sales tax rate 9%. Items sold by nonprofit or charitable organizations are exempt from sales tax.

Non-Resident State Income Tax

South Carolina, lacking reciprocal agreements, requires residents working in other states and non-residents in South Carolina to pay the higher of the two states' tax rates.

STATE INCOME TAX

South Dakota

The Mount Rushmore State has no income tax but high property taxes compared to other states.

South Dakota is home to the famous Mount Rushmore monument, creating the nickname the Mount Rushmore state.

"South Dakota does not have a state income tax."

Adding to its allure, South Dakota doesn't impose taxes on personal income, capital gains, estates, or inheritances.

Property Tax
In South Dakota, with an effective property tax rate of 1.17% and a median home value of $338,388.89, homeowners face an annual tax bill of approximately $3,953.73.

State and Local Sales Tax
South Dakota residents are subject to a 4.2% sales tax rate as of July 1, 2023, which dropped from 4.5%. In addition, municipalities can impose an additional 4.5% tax, making the total combined rate nearly 9%.

Non-Resident State Income Tax
South Dakota has no state income tax. South Dakota residents working in other states pay income taxes to those states. Non-residents working in South Dakota pay income taxes to their own states.

Tennessee

The Volunteer State has no state income tax and low property taxes, but high sales taxes.

Tennessee gets its nickname from residents playing a key role in the War of 1812, with thousands of volunteers joining frontline efforts.

Tennessee is one of only seven states that doesn't impose taxes on personal income, capital gains, estates, or inheritances.

"Tennessee doesn't have a state income tax."

Property Tax
In Tennessee, with an effective property tax rate of 0.67% and a median home value of $349,375.90, homeowners face an annual tax bill of approximately $2,332.37.

State and Local Sales Tax
Tennessee imposes a 7% state sales tax rate on most goods and services. In addition, localities can assess another 2.75% in taxes, bringing the max sales tax rate to 9.75%. Tennessee holds some of the nation's highest sales tax rates, which helps offset lost revenue from no individual income tax.

Non-Resident State Income Tax

Tennessee has no state income tax. Tennessee residents working in other states pay income taxes to those states. Non-residents working in Tennessee pay income taxes to their own states.

STATE INCOME TAX

Texas

The Lone Star State has no state income tax but levies the nation's sixth-highest property tax rates.

Texas's nickname comes from the Lone Star Flag, which was adopted shortly after Texas became independent from Mexico.

In line with its independent spirit, Texas doesn't impose taxes on personal income, capital gains, estates, or inheritances. However, residents do have the responsibility of paying sales tax and property taxes.

"Texas does not have a state income tax."

Property Tax

In Texas, with an effective property tax rate of 1.68% and a median home value of $350,000.62, homeowners face an annual tax bill of approximately $5,870.39.

State and Local Sales Tax

Texas imposes a state sales tax rate of 6.25%, with localities able to levy an additional 2%. This brings the maximum combined sales tax rate to 8.25%. Groceries are specifically excluded from sales tax. However, nonfood items bought at grocery stores are still subject to sales tax.

Non-Resident State Income Tax

Texas has no state income tax. Texas residents working in other states pay income taxes to those states. Non-residents working in Texas pay income taxes to their own states

STATE INCOME TAX

Utah

The Beehive State has low property tax rates but a high combined sales tax rate.

Utah's nickname comes from its historical association with the beehive as a symbol of industry and hard work. Early Mormon pioneers settled in Utah in the 1800s and likened their collaborative efforts to bees working together for the common good.

Today, Utah uses a flat tax rate of 4.65%, which applies to ordinary income as well as capital gains.

The state provides several tax credits to help reduce your tax liability. One of these is the taxpayer tax credit, valued at $831 for each taxpayer. Consequently, if you're married and filing jointly, you can claim $1,662. Additionally, Utah offers a personal exemption for each dependent you list on your federal tax return. For the year 2023, this exemption amount is $1,802, and it's indexed to adjust for inflation.

> *"Utah levies a flat tax rate of 4.65%, regardless of filing status or income level."*

Property Tax
In Utah, with an effective property tax rate of 0.57% and a median home value of $431,500.00, homeowners face an annual tax bill of approximately $2,460.97.

State and Local Sales Tax
Utah's base sales tax is 6.1%, including a mandatory 1.25% local add-on surcharge. Reduced rates are in place for essentials such as food and residential energy, taxed at 3% and 2.85%, respectively. In addition, local Utah governments can impose additional sales taxes — up to 4.2% — for specific services like transit, roads, arts, and rural hospitals, each with its own designated rate. When these taxes are combined, Park City holds the distinction of having the highest total sales tax in Utah at 9.05%

Non-Resident State Income Tax

Utah does not have reciprocal agreements, so residents working in other states and non-residents in Utah are subject to the higher of the two states' tax rates.

STATE INCOME TAX

Vermont

High property and income tax rates in the Green Mountain State drive a heavy overall tax burden.

Named after "Les Monts Verts," which means Green Mountains in French, as a tribute to the stunning 67 mountains that define its landscape.

Vermont follows a progressive tax system with a top tax bracket of 8.75%.

But residents of Vermont have a few different ways to lower taxable income. First, taxpayers can take a standard deduction. These amounts were $6,500 for single filers and married individuals filing separately, $9,800 for heads of households, and $13,050 for married couples filing jointly in 2022. The finalized 2023 standard deduction amounts have not yet been released.

Second, Vermont's allows a personal exemption of $4,500 for each taxpayer and dependent, which means if you're married filing jointly, you can claim $9,000.

Additionally, Vermont taxpayers can exclude a portion of Social Security income from taxation and take additional deductions for dependents, student loan interest, and military income.

Vermont Income Tax Rates

Rates apply to income between that bracket and the next highest bracket

2023 Tax Rates	Single Taxpayer	Married Filing Jointly	Married Filing Separately	Head of Household
3.35%	$0	$0	$0	$0
6.60%	$45,400	$75,850	$37,925	$60,850
7.60%	$110,500	$183,400	$91,700	$157,150
8.75%	$229,550	$279,450	$139,729	$254,500

Capital Gains Tax

Vermont taxes short-term capital gains and long-term capital gains held for up to three years as ordinary income and they are all taxed at the same rates. Taxpayers are allowed to exclude up to 40% of gains from certain assets held more than three years or up to $5,000 of capital gains are excluded from taxation.

Estate and Inheritance Taxes

In 2023, Vermont's estate tax exemption is $5 million. Most Vermont residents won't face estate taxes unless their estate's value exceeds this amount. For estates worth over $5 million, only the excess is taxed at a 16% rate. For instance, an $8 million estate would have a tax liability of $480,000 on the extra $3 million. On the other hand, Vermont doesn't have an inheritance tax, which means heirs can benefit from significant tax savings.

Property Tax

In Vermont, with an effective property tax rate of 1.83% and a median home value of $339,969.84, homeowners face an annual tax bill of approximately $6,207.08.

State and Local Sales Tax

Vermont imposes a 6% state sales tax rate. Localities can levy an additional 1% on most purchases. Vermont also has a 9% meals and rooms tax, which applies to restaurant meals, lodging, and meeting rooms in hotels. Alcoholic beverages in restaurants are taxed at a rate of 10%.

Non-Resident State Income Tax

Vermont, without reciprocal agreements, requires residents working in other states and non-residents in Vermont to pay the higher of the two states' tax rates.

STATE INCOME TAX

Virginia

The Old Dominion State has above-average income taxes for some but low property taxes.

Known as the Old Dominion State, Virginia was England's first overseas territory.

In addition to its historic status, the state has a graduated-rate tax system, with rates ranging from 2% to 5.75%, which apply to ordinary income as well as capital gains.

Virginia's standard deduction is $8,000 for individual filers and $16,000 for married couples filing jointly, with an additional $3,000 deduction per eligible dependent, up to $6,000. Every filer, including spouses and dependents, receives a $930 tax exemption, with an extra $800 exemption for those over 65 or legally blind.

Another positive aspect to note is that Virginia does not impose estate or inheritance taxes.

Virginia Income Tax Rates

Rates apply to income between each bracket and the next higher bracket

2023 Tax Rates	Tax Bracket
2.00%	$0
3.00%	$3,000
5.00%	$5,000
5.75%	$17,000

Property Tax

In Virginia, with an effective property tax rate of 0.87% and a median home value of $385,038.11, homeowners face an annual tax bill of approximately $3,367.61.

State and Local Sales Tax

The state sales tax rate in Virginia is 5.3%, with localities able to levy a combined tax rate of up to 7%. James City County, Williamsburg, and York County all currently assess a sales tax rate of 7%. Food and personal hygiene items are capped at a 1% sales tax rate. Vehicle sales tax rates can vary by county.

Non-Resident State Income Tax

Virginia's reciprocal agreements with Kentucky, Maryland, the District of Columbia, Pennsylvania, and West Virginia enable residents of these areas working in Virginia, and Virginia residents working in these areas, to pay state taxes only to their respective home states.

STATE INCOME TAX

Washington

The Evergreen State taxes only income from long-term capital gains over $250,000.

Washington earned its nickname from the plentiful evergreen forests that pepper its landscape. The residents don't just revel in the state's breathtaking beauty, but also enjoy the benefit of not having to pay any individual income tax.

However, it's not all tax-free – they are required to pay a 7% tax on their capital gains income over $250,000, regardless of filing status.

"Washington levies a flat tax rate of 7% on capital gains only."

Estate and Inheritance Taxes

In Washington, estates valued at $2,193,000 or less are exempt from estate tax. For those exceeding this amount, the tax rates vary between 10% and 20%. However, Washington doesn't have an inheritance tax, which means heirs can benefit from significant tax savings.

Property Tax

In Washington, with an effective property tax rate of 0.87% and a median home value of $549,990.32, homeowners face an annual tax bill of approximately $4,802.79.

State and Local Sales Tax

Washington state imposes a 6.5% sales tax rate. With localities able to levy an additional 4.1%, residents may be required to pay up to 10.6% on purchases. Additionally, Washington charges extra tax on lodging, with the rate varying by quarter and municipality.

Non-Resident State Income Tax

Washington State does not levy state income tax on earned income. Residents working in other states must pay income taxes to those states, and non-residents working in

Washington pay income taxes to their respective home states.

West Virginia

The Mountain State, which has low property tax rates, lowered income tax rates this year.

West Virginia, aptly nicknamed the Mountain State, is fully nestled within the Appalachian Mountain region.
Its residents enjoy the bonus of moderate income taxes, ranging from 2.36% to 5.12%, which apply to ordinary income as well as capital gains.

West Virginia does not have a standard deduction, but the state does allow each taxpayer to claim a personal exemption of $2,000 for both themselves and any eligible dependents. This means that a couple filing their taxes jointly could claim a total exemption of $4,000.

Another advantage is that West Virginia doesn't have estate or inheritance taxes.

West Virginia Income Tax

Rates apply to income between each
bracket and the next higher bracket

2023 Tax Rates	Tax Bracket
2.36%	$0
3.15%	$10,000
3.54%	$25,000
4.72%	$40,000
5.12%	$60,000

Property Tax

In West Virginia, with an effective property tax rate of 0.57%
and a median home value of $214,446.21, homeowners face
an annual tax bill of approximately $1,217.47.

State and Local Sales Tax

West Virginia has a 6% state sales tax rate, with localities
able to assess an additional 1%. This makes the combined
maximum rate 7%. Most counties choose to levy the
additional 1%.

Non-Resident State Income Tax

West Virginia, with reciprocal agreements with Kentucky,
Maryland, Ohio, Pennsylvania, and Virginia, allows residents
of these states working in West Virginia, and West Virginia
residents working in these states, to pay state taxes only to
their respective home states.

Wisconsin

The Badger State allows deductions on long-term capital gains income.

Wisconsin earned its nickname from early miners who lived in hillside burrows like badgers, symbolizing the state's industrious spirit.

The state uses a graduated-rate income tax system, with rates ranging from 3.54% to 7.64%.

Wisconsin allows its taxpayers to claim a standard deduction: $12,760 for single filers, $23,620 for married couples filing jointly, $11,220 for married individuals filing separately, and $16,480 for heads of households.

Additionally, residents can claim a $700 personal exemption, which doubles to $1,400 for married couples filing jointly, with each dependent also qualifying for an additional $700 exemption.

Another advantage is that Wisconsin doesn't have estate or inheritance taxes.

Wisconsin Income Tax Rates

Rates apply to income between that bracket and the next highest bracket

2023 Tax Rates	Single Taxpayer	Married Filing Jointly	Married Filing Separately	Head of Household
3.54%	$0	$0	$0	$0
4.65%	$13,810	$18,420	$9,210	$13,810
5.30%	$27,630	$36,840	$18,420	$27,630
7.65%	$304,170	$405,550	$202,780	$304,170

Capital Gains Tax

Wisconsin taxes capital gains at ordinary income rates but allows a deduction of 30% (or 60% for farm asset sales) on long-term capital gains.

Property Tax

In Wisconsin, with an effective property tax rate of 1.61% and a median home value of $264,923.47, homeowners face an annual tax bill of approximately $4,265.39.

State and Local Sales Tax

Wisconsin currently levies a 5% state sales tax rate. Individual counties can impose another 1.75% local tax on purchases. This makes the maximum combined rate 6.75%, which is low compared to many other states. Groceries, prescription medicine, and manufactured homes are excluded from sales tax.

Non-Resident State Income Tax

Wisconsin's reciprocal agreements with Illinois, Indiana, Kentucky, and Michigan mean residents of these states working in Wisconsin, and Wisconsin residents working in these states, pay state taxes only to their respective home states.

Wyoming

The Equality State has no state income tax and the sixth-lowest overall tax burden in the nation.

Wyoming, known as the Equality State, earned its nickname by being the first U.S. territory to grant women the right to vote in 1869, well ahead of the 19th Amendment in 1920.

> *"Wyoming does not have a state income tax."*

Residents also enjoy financial benefits like low sales and property taxes, and no personal income, capital gains, estate, or inheritance taxes.

Property Tax

In Wyoming, with an effective property tax rate of 0.56% and a median home value of $274,432.34, homeowners face an annual tax bill of approximately $1,524.60.

State and Local Sales Tax

Wyoming imposes a state sales tax rate of 4%. Localities are also capped at an additional tax rate of 2%. This brings the maximum state and local sales tax to 6%. Groceries purchased with food stamps, prescription medicine, and medical devices are exempt from state and local sales tax.

Non-Resident State Income Tax

Wyoming, having no state income tax, means residents working in other states pay income tax to those states, while non-residents in Wyoming pay their home state taxes.

Apprentice to **Giants**

The pioneers who built the foundations of investing

During my career, I've been fortunate to receive guidance from some of the most influential figures in investment theory and management. Their enduring contributions are risk and return, diversification, tax optimization and behavioral finance.

Risk and Return
Harry Markowitz

Harry received the Nobel Prize for his pioneering work in modern portfolio theory, which he first published as a graduate student in 1952. He was in his eighties when I worked with him, and just as sharp.

Harry's groundbreaking idea was to rigorously correlate risk and return – moving investing from the bar room to the computer room. He developed what is now called the efficient frontier (then the "Markowitz frontier") – an approach to building

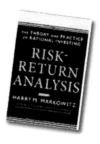

portfolios that produce the maximum return with the minimum risk.

A driving factor is holding a broad spectrum of assets – diversification. On average, stocks with similar risk will yield a similar expected return. But, if you only invest in a few stocks, your actual return will be more volatile than if you invest in many stocks. If you invest in just a few, you can expect the same return but with higher risk. This is called "uncompensated risk" – you're taking risk without being paid for it.

Over 60 years later, modern portfolio theory remains at the heart of most disciplined investing programs today.

Diversification
John Bogle

Jack founded Vanguard and single-handedly dragged a recalcitrant investment community towards index investing. As a result of decades of steadfast advocacy of his heretical ideas, Vanguard is now the largest consumer asset manager in the world.

I met with Jack numerous times before his passing and put his advice to work at my own firm, Personal Capital, which became one of the largest independent investment advisors in the country. Of course, we only managed billions of dollars while Jack managed trillions!

Jack pushed Harry's concept of diversification to its logical extreme. His idea was as simple as it was revolutionary – instead of owning many stocks, own them all. Thus, to the vexation of old-time stock brokers and overconfident fund managers, the index fund was born.

The reality is that, over the long term, it is nearly impossible to beat the market – a fact confirmed by study after study. The prudent approach is to diversify, be patient, and let the market work for you.

Harry pointed the way and Jack built the path.

Tax Optimization
Mike Chipman

Mike was the original developer of TurboTax, one of the earliest and most successful examples of personal financial software. During the nineties, I ran his company and he introduced me to the art and science of software programming.

His insight was simple: software could be used to make financial work easier and to minimize income taxes. Follow all the rules, but be smart about it. After all, it's not what you earn, it's what you keep that counts.

We've come a long way since the early desktop versions of TurboTax. Tax optimization of investments has become a science, with strategies like loss harvesting, gain deferral, asset location, charitable giving and effective use of tax-advantaged accounts, like 401k's, IRAs, Roths, 529s, SEPs, DAFs and others.

For 30 years, I've worked at the crossroads of technology and finance. Mike showed me what you can achieve by combining these two pursuits – even 30 years ago when personal computers were just tinker toys.

Behavioral Finance
Shlomo Benartzi

Shlomo is a student of human financial behavior and co-authored the bible of retirement savings, *Save More Tomorrow,* along with Nobel laureate Richard Thaler. Some years later, Shlomo and I worked together to investigate the impact of mobile technology on financial habits.

Thaler and Daniel Kahneman, another Nobel recipient, fathered the field of behavioral finance – the study of how people actually behave with their money and how to "nudge" them towards healthier behaviors.

Save More Tomorrow is an ingenious approach to increasing participation in 401k retirement savings plans. Instead of exhorting employees to increase their 401k contributions today, which would reduce their take-home pay, ask them to commit  today to automatically increase their contributions a year from now. By eliminating the short-term pain, many more households embrace the journey to effective investing for retirement.

Behaviorists call this a cognitive bias – specifically, the "future-self continuity" bias – where today's desires overwhelm tomorrow's well-being.

Behavioral economists put practice ahead of theory. What good is a solid investment philosophy if people don't use it? More important than *how* you invest, is *that* you invest.

A Personal Note

I have enjoyed writing this book and hope it is helpful. I acknowledge Anna-Louise Jackson, who wrote the tax advantaged accounts chapter, and my editor, Catheryn Keegan, who wrote the state tax chapter.

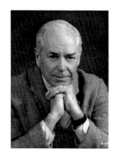

I also acknowledge my father, Dr. William Harris, who is the biggest influence on my life. Throughout his 60-year career as an orthopedic surgeon and clinician-scientist, he conquered two worldwide diseases and saved or improved the lives of millions. You can read the gripping story of that conquest in his book, *Vanishing Bone.* Whether at the bedside or the bench (the hospital or the research lab), his driving force was and is (he is 96 years old and still writing) restless innovation.